CAN

3 STEP PROGRAM

This book is about letting go of the things we can't change, focusing on things we can change and serving by way of our gifts.

This book is a testimonial of what our lives were like before we let go and the changes that took place overnight the moment we did.

Courtenay British Columbia Canada
2013

Note for Librarians: A cataloguing record for this book is available from Library and Archives Canada at www.collectionscanada.ca/amicus/index-e.html

Library and Archives Canada Cataloguing in Publication

Porcher, Carey, 1970-, author
      Can I change it? : 3 step program / Carey Porcher.

Issued in print and electronic formats.
ISBN 978-0-9919181-0-2 (pbk.).--ISBN 978-0-9919181-1-9 (pdf)

      1. Change (Psychology). 2. Self-actualization (Psychology).
I. Title.

BF637.C4P63 2013   158.1   C2013-902412-3
                                             C2013-902413-1

ISBN – 978-0-9919181-0-2

                    Printed in Canada
                          ♻
                    on recycled paper

FIRST CHOICE BOOKS
                 www.firstchoicebooks.ca
                      Victoria, BC

                 10 9 8 7 6 5 4 3 2 1

CAN I CHANGE IT?

Introduction

Is it possible we spend as much as 90% of our day focused on things we can't change?

How much time do we spend focusing on past or future events we have little to no control over?

How much time do we spend trying to change or control other people while our lives remain in complete shambles?

How much of our day is spent living in anger, fear and resentment towards others?

What if we made a decision to completely let go of the past and make today the first day of the rest of our lives?

What if today we made a decision to focus only on things we can change?

Most of us have come to realize life is short, life is difficult and we can't take anything with us when we go.

Most of us have come to realize we can't change the past, we can't guarantee the future and today is all that we have.

Most of us have come to realize we've all made mistakes and today is the first day of the rest of our lives.

Agnostics and atheists alike have come to realize they can throw the dice but certainly don't determine how they land.

This book is about letting go of the past, focusing on things we can change and serving by way of our gifts.

This book is a testimonial of what our lives were like before we let go and the changes that took place overnight the moment we did.

Today is the first day of the rest of our lives!

<u>Forward</u>

We are a small group of people whose lives have changed overnight by a simple process of letting go of the past, focusing on things we can change and serving by way of our gifts.

The main purpose of this simple, repetitive, alphabetical, glossary style book is to show others how they too can change their lives overnight no matter how hopeless or discouraging things seem in the present moment.

We hope the following pages are so simple and straight forward, no further diligence is necessary.

These simple, quantifiable, real life examples are scientific, useful, and therapeutic, and focus on serving our fellows.

We hope by sharing our before and after experiences, you will find a level of familiarity and humility that will allow you to find the courage to let go, get honest and change the course of your life starting today.

We are very interested in hearing from people who have read this book and are making profound changes in their lives and the lives of others. You can reach us at www.canichangeit.com. Please pass this book on to someone you know who needs it more than you. As of today, we no longer go through life as a single braided cord.

Today is the first day of the rest of our lives!

Disease of Entitlement

In clinical psychology and psychiatry terms, Entitlement is "an unrealistic right to demand lifelong reimbursement."

In the line of service, we've come to believe entitlement is a disease not yet labelled or diagnosed and is comparable with cocaine and heroin addiction for many reasons.

In both cases:

- ✓ do anything to get what they want
- ✓ extremely costly
- ✓ will stop at nothing to get more
- ✓ never enough
- ✓ unmanageable
- ✓ destroys families
- ✓ sabotage's relationships
- ✓ can lead to premature death
- ✓ often difficult to detect

We've come to believe that those with the disease of entitlement must be treated in the same way we treat drug addiction, as neither group cares about anyone other than themselves, while in active addiction. These groups will stop at nothing to get what they want, when they want, or how they want it.

We've come to believe people looking for a hand up vs. a hand out are not one in the same group. We believe these groups must be clearly identified when assessing service requirements.

The good news is, we know both groups can experience overnight miracles if they are willing to let go, get honest and focus on serving others...not just themselves.

We've all made mistakes. Spiritual progress is the key...not spiritual perfection!

Today is the first day of the rest of our lives!

Carey's Story

At 40 years of age I found myself living in a van, staying warm at libraries and soup kitchens, and surviving on welfare cheques. I had lost my dreams, my companies, my animals, my family, my assets, and everything of "value". There was no point carrying on other than the fact I was a coward and didn't have the courage to take my own life. I was stuck.

It was Christmas day, I was 40 years of age, my family was gone and I had simply had enough. For the first time I had lost the will to live. The question was how do I end my life?

Over the next few years I found myself on the doorsteps of Churches, Alcoholics Anonymous meetings and the library, soaking up all the information I could find on religion, philosophy, self-help and everything in between.

The same message kept reappearing in religious doctrine and AA and the message was simple and direct, "surrender your will or perish".

Although I didn't quite understand it or how to accomplish it, I knew **my way didn't work** and I was sick and tired of hanging on.

One day I simply let go with the realization I can't change the past and created a list of things in my life I could change...the results were unbelievable!

Not only had I come to feel a level of peace, joy, and love but looking back I realized over 90% of my days were focused on things I couldn't change. This ranged from past and future events, to watching TV, to wishing my family, friends, and the world around me could be different.

It immediately occurred to me that if I was focusing 90% of my day on things I couldn't change how about the people I came into contact with on a daily basis? Was it possible there were others like me, totally stuck; focusing the majority of their thoughts and energy on things they couldn't change?

Today I've let go of the past. Today I focus on things I can change without getting attached to the outcome. Today I live and serve by way of my gifts. Today I'm able to get honest and find humility in almost every situation. Today I live in acceptance, gratitude, surrender and service.

Today my purpose is to share where I was before letting go and the changes that took place the moment I did.

3 Step Program

We let go, focused on things we can change and served others

1)   *We let go* - We spend 30 minutes writing down all the things in our lives we can't change that we must let go of. We become aware of what these are and why we can't change them. This step is about letting go of the things we can't change both today and moving forward.

2)   *Focused on things we can change* - We spend 30 minutes writing down all the things we can and must change. We get absolutely clear about what we want, the reasons we want them and when we want to achieve them by. This is a critical step as thoughts become things. All the greatest achievements started as an idea. Today we know life without goals is a life without purpose. This step is about creating purpose.

3)   *Served others* - We spend 30 minutes filling out a gifting sheet identifying our unique proprietary gifts. We learn that when we live and serve by way of these gifts we experience levels of peace, joy and happiness. We come to realize most mental illness such as depression, anxiety, addiction, co-dependency & entitlement all have one common denominator...focus on self. Today we know the moment we take focus off self, these diseases slowly dissolve.

** Today is the first day of the rest of our lives! - We've applied this to every page as it's critical to a happy and healthy life moving forward. Focusing on things we can't change over long periods of time is the root cause of depression and many other serious mental illnesses. The past does not equal the future unless we let it. Once we let go, today truly is the first day of the rest of our lives.

Today is the first day of the rest of our lives!

Acknowledgements

I would like to express my deepest gratitude to those individuals and groups who have dedicated their lives to serving their fellows. From AA to Anthony Robbins...Thank You!

I would also like to thank the many people before me who paved the way with many of the principles and philosophies set forth in this book.

I would like to thank Philip, Amy and Darren Chen for entering my family's life and enabling me to write this book.

Above all I want to thank my son's, Max and Jimmy, and my daughter Victoria, who loved, supported and encouraged me through my worst times... I love you guys!

I would like to thank those who continually demonstrated unconditional love when I needed it most; Janice Porcher, Bob Verret, Dali & Jin Lin, Alisa Hooper...Thank You!

Special thanks to Kathy Porcher, Jane Cunningham and Tina Storms who cared for the kids when the chips were down.

Last but not least, thanks to those who have been with me over the course of the years and whose names I have failed to mention.

<u>Acceptance</u>

YESTERDAY

Yesterday our hearts and minds were closed. We listened if and when it benefitted us. We had our own ideas. We were often intolerant of others and new ideas. It was our way or no way. Closed minded thinking came at a serious cost. All we knew was that our way didn't work.

We let go, focused on things we could change and served others

TODAY

Today we know we roll the dice, but certainly don't determine how they land. Today we know we're powerless over our birth, our death and most things in between. Today we accept the fact that life is short, life is difficult and we can't take anything with us when we go. Today we accept we can't change the past or guarantee the future...today is all that we have. Today we know the only people we can change is ourselves. Today we've reopened our hearts and minds. Today we've learned to accept life on life's terms. Today we accept people, places and things as they are. Today we know acceptance is a key to a happy life. Today we've learned to love and accept our enemies even if we have to love them from afar.

*Principle- Accept life on life's terms.

Today is the first day of the rest of our lives!

Accountability

YESTERDAY

Yesterday it was never our fault. We didn't do anything wrong! We were misunderstood. We were in the wrong place at the wrong time. People simply didn't understand us.

We let go, focused on things we could change and served others

TODAY

Today we own our own stuff. Today we're the first to admit when we're wrong. Today we know rigorous self-honesty is the only way to free ourselves from the bondage of our past. Today we know self-honesty leads to humility. Today we know self-honesty and humility are the foundations from which all love, forgiveness, kindness and mercy grow. Today we've taken a searching and moral inventory of ourselves and reached out to all the people we had harmed and let them know we are sorry. Today we've cleared away the wreckage of our past and live life to the fullest each and every day.

*Principle- Rigorous self-honesty is mandatory.

Today is the first day of the rest of our lives!

Acid/Alkalinity

YESTERDAY

Yesterday acid played an active role in our lives. Stress, pressure, negativity, white flour, white sugar, white salt, caffeine, alcohol, tobacco...we were highly acidic. As our bodies became toxic, our minds became toxic.

We let go, focused on things we could change and served others

TODAY

Today we understand acid is the root cause of many human ailments such as strokes, heart attacks, cancers and much more. Today we understand most diseases such as cancer struggle to mutate in an alkaline body. Today we keep our bodies alkalized. Today we've learned to live alkaline lives and eat alkaline foods. Today we know lemons, greens, and watermelon top the list when cleansing and alkalizing the body. Today we know a healthy body makes for a healthy mind. Today we work towards letting go of acid forming foods and living happier, healthier lives.

*Principle- Cancer struggles to mutate in an alkaline body.

Today is the first day of the rest of our lives!

<u>Actions</u>

YESTERDAY

Yesterday negative thoughts led to negative actions. Negative actions led to negative habits. Negative habits led to negative lives. Nothing complicated here.

We let go, focused on things we could change and served others

TODAY

Today we've cultivated the soil. Today we've replanted healthy thoughts. Today we know what we want, why we want it, and when we want it by. Today we know healthy thoughts and actions act as the rudder that directs the course of our lives. Today we know our gifts and how to best direct them.

Principle- Actions act as the rudder that directs the course of our lives.

Today is the first day of the rest of our lives!

<u>Addiction</u>

YESTERDAY

Yesterday our focus was self-gratification. Food, coffee, cigarettes, alcohol, drugs, sex, control...personal entitlement! Self-will had run riot. It was all about us. It was never enough. We knew our ways didn't work...we simply couldn't stop!

We let go, focused on things we could change and served others

TODAY

Today we found the courage to let go **absolutely;** knowing half measures availed us nothing. Today we've **unconditionally** surrendered; convinced our best efforts weren't enough. Today we choose life over death. Today we work towards daily progress...not perfection! Today we know yesterday's liabilities are our greatest assets when serving others. Today we use our experience, strength and hope to serve others. Today we lead with a sense of humility, love and encouragement.

*Principle- Half measures availed us nothing.

Today is the first day of the rest of our lives!

Admit When We're Wrong

YESTERDAY

Yesterday being right was more important than being honest. Yesterday being right was more important than being happy. Yesterday being right was more important than maintaining happy healthy relationships with the ones we love. Being right cost us friendships, family and marriages.

We let go, focused on things we could change and served others

TODAY

Today we found the courage to get rigorously self-honest. This was the most difficult and critical step in the process. Without this step, there was no chance of recovery. When done successfully, this produced the gift of humility. From humility sprang love, forgiveness, compassion, kindness and a willingness to help others. Humility has reopened our hearts and minds. Today we have the courage to be the first to admit when we are wrong. Today we come from a place of love and encouragement. Today we experience love, peace and joy like never before. Today we've reached out to all those we had harmed and made amends to them all. Today it's about being happy...not being right!

Principle- Focus on being happy...not being right!

Today is the first day of the rest of our lives!

Adversity

YESTERDAY

Yesterday we made poor choices. We crossed lines we never thought we would cross. For many we could never go back to living normal lives. We had passed the point of no return. We lied to others but couldn't lie to ourselves. We lived with guilt, shame, remorse and depression and often much worse. We were enslaved by our past.

We let go, focused on things we could change and served others

TODAY

Today we possess wisdom. Today we know yesterday's liabilities are our biggest asset. Today we know there are few lessons in success. Today we know every adversity carries with it the seed to a greater benefit. Today we know success comes from making the right decision, the right decision comes from experience and experience comes from making the wrong decision! Today we know nothing in life happens so bad we can't either laugh at it or learn something from it. Today we know there is no substitute for experience. Today with every adversity we ask ourselves; "What can we learn from this?"

*Principle- There are few lessons in success.

Today is the first day of the rest of our lives!

All Things Decay

YESTERDAY

Yesterday stuff was our objective. More cars, houses, boats...it was all about acquiring stuff. The more we had, the better we were supposed to feel...right? The more we had, the better we looked...right? Money and materialism took priority over people and relationships...right? If we were right, why were we miserable? Why did we feel like we were drowning?

We let go, focused on things we could change and served others

TODAY

Today we know everything decays. Today we know the illusion of attachment is the "stuff" that kept us enslaved. Today we know we can't take even one penny with us at the time of our death. Today we know being the richest man in the graveyard is not our goal! Today we know wisdom is the greatest asset one can possess. Today we know it's in giving that we receive. Today we know it's about needing less, not wanting more! Today we know the best things in life are free. Today we are free.

*Principle- Being the richest man in the graveyard is not our goal.

Today is the first day of the rest of our lives!

<u>Anger</u>

YESTERDAY

Yesterday we lived in expectation and entitlement. When we didn't get what we wanted, when we wanted, how we wanted it, we got angry. Nothing complicated here. Anger, stress, frustration and disappointment were all code names for fear. Our fear led to anger. Our anger led to hate. Our hate led to suffering. It was all about fear!

We let go, focused on things we could change and served others

TODAY

Today we've let go of our expectations and entitlements. Today we know we can't change the past or guarantee the future...today is all that we have. Today we accept life on life's terms knowing we may roll the dice but certainly don't determine how they land. Today we accept people, places and things as they are; knowing we can only change ourselves. Today we no longer get attached to the outcome in any given situation. Today we know when we open our hearts and minds and stop forcing our will on others, we find levels of peace and joy we never thought possible. Today we lead with love and encouragement.

*Principle- Fear leads to anger. Anger leads to hate. Hate leads to suffering.

Today is the first day of the rest of our lives!

Attitude of Gratitude

YESTERDAY

Yesterday we lived in expectation and entitlement. We focused on what we didn't have. For many, it didn't matter what we had...it was never enough! Habitually we focused on the bottom 10% of everything...not the top 10%! We woke up wanting more. More, more, more was our motto!

We let go, focused on things we could change and served others

TODAY

Today we know when we're grateful, we're rich. Today we know we can't be grateful and depressed at the same time. Today we start each day with a list of things we are grateful for. Today we focus on what we have vs. what we don't have. Today we know everything we have is a privilege...not a right! Today we focus on the top 10%...not the bottom 10%. Today it's about needing less...not wanting more! Today we live with an attitude of gratitude.

*Principle- When we're grateful we're rich.

Today is the first day of the rest of our lives!

Attraction...Not Promotion!

YESTERDAY

Yesterday we preached one message and demonstrated another. We made promises we never kept. We told people what we wanted them to hear. Over time, we started believing our own press. We couldn't understand why no one trusted us.

We let go, focused on things we could change and served others

TODAY

Today we lead by example. Today we treat others the way we want to be treated. Today we lead with love and encouragement. Today we keep an open heart and an open mind. Today we speak less and do more. Today we force our will on no one! Today we focus on changing ourselves rather than changing others. Today we live by way of attraction...not promotion.

*Principle- Today we lead by example.

Today is the first day of the rest of our lives!

Bad to Worse to Better

YESTERDAY

Yesterday when things got bad we panicked. When things got worse we quit. We had little faith. Fear got the best of us. Short delays ended up as failures.

We let go, focused on things we could change and served others

TODAY

Today we know things often go from bad to worse before getting better. Today we have faith in a power greater than ourselves. Today we know God's delays are not God's denials. Today we know a planted seed grows on God's time...not ours! Today we have the patience to weather the storms knowing "this too shall pass". Today we know we roll the dice but someone or something else determines how they land. Today we accept life on life's terms.

*Principle- God's delays are not God's denials.

Today is the first day of the rest of our lives!

<u>Balance</u>

YESTERDAY

Yesterday we had very little balance or routine. Everything we did, we did to the extreme. We burned ourselves out. We burned the people around us out. We were "all in" regardless of what we did. In most cases, we were strong out of the gate but weak finishers. Moderation was in short supply.

We let go, focused on things we could change and served others

TODAY

Today we've learned the importance of balance, routine and moderation. Today we know routine is a key to a happy, healthy, productive life. Today we live simple lives. Today we live one day at a time. Today we accept life on life's terms. Today we get still by way of prayer and meditation. Today we know getting still opens the door to inspiration, insight and wisdom.

*Principle- Routine is a key to a happy, healthy, productive life.

Today is the first day of the rest of our lives!

Boundaries

YESTERDAY

Yesterday we were a direct reflection of our peer group. We became the people we associated with. We became infected by letting the wrong people in. Soon we infected the people that let us in. Without boundaries nothing was sacred.

We let go, focused on things we could change and served others

TODAY

Today we maintain two very simple boundaries. First; we treat others the way we want to be treated and expect the same in return. Second; trust and respect are mandatory. Today those who fall short of our boundaries we love from afar. Today we know it only takes one bad apple to destroy the entire barrel. Today we walk our journey with other likeminded givers or we walk it alone.

*Principle- Fellowship with givers...not takers!

Today is the first day of the rest of our lives!

Can I Change It?

YESTERDAY

Yesterday we focused up to 90% of our thoughts on things we couldn't change. Changing people, changing the past...the insanity went on! Our lives were a mess yet we still found the time to condemn, criticize and complain. We weren't happy, our lives were falling apart and still we hung on to our old ideas right till the bitter end. For many of us we were introduced to the serenity prayer; "God, grant us the serenity to accept the things we cannot change, the courage to change the things we can and the wisdom to know the difference". There was hope after all.

We let go, focused on things we could change and served others

TODAY

Today with every situation, we ask ourselves one simple question; can I change it? If the answer is no, we disengage immediately...immediately! If the answer is yes, we ask ourselves if it's something we want to change. If the answer is no, we disengage immediately! Today we know what we want, why we want it and when we want to achieve it by. Today we know obstacles are what we see when we take our eyes off our goals. Today we've taken the time to learn our gifts and live and serve by way of our gifts. Today we know the only people we can change is ourselves. Today we stay focused on the things we can change.

*Principle- #1 question- Can I change it?

Today is the first day of the rest of our lives!

<u>Change</u>

YESTERDAY

Yesterday we hung on to our old ideas and beliefs. We guarded them with our lives as we worked so hard to acquire them. Few, if any, were still working. We were miserable! We so wanted to get to second base but wouldn't take our foot off first...we were stuck!

We let go, focused on things we could change and served others

TODAY

Today we found the courage to let go absolutely knowing our old ways didn't work. Today we know life is short and we're not here long. Today we know we roll the dice but don't determine how they land. Today we know everything decays. Today we believe in a power greater than ourselves. Today we live one day at a time, in acceptance and gratitude, knowing every moment is a privilege...not a right! Today we know the only constant in life is change. Today we accept life on life's terms...not ours! Today we focus on things we can change!

*Principle- The only constant in life is change.

Today is the first day of the rest of our lives!

Choosing Friends Wisely

YESTERDAY

Yesterday we let the wrong people in. Poor choices in friends cost some of us our lives. We were surrounded by takers. Over time we became one. Nothing complicated here.

We let go, focused on things we could change and served others

TODAY

Today we walk alone rather than let the wrong people in. Today we choose our friends wisely. Today we associate with givers not takers. Today we find likeminded people who focus on serving others...not just themselves! Today we know choosing the right people can be the difference between life and death. Today we associate with people we trust and respect who share our motto, "help each other don't hurt each other". Today we know it only takes one sick person to destroy our entire lives...just one!

*Principle- Choose your friends wisely!

Today is the first day of the rest of our lives!

Crabology

YESTERDAY

Yesterday we were like crabs in a pot. If we saw one trying to crawl out or get ahead we pulled them down to our level. Like crabs in a pot we didn't want to get left behind.

We let go, focused on things we could change and served others

TODAY

Today we know it isn't necessary to blow out the others persons light in order to let our own light shine. Today we lift those around us by leading with love and encouragement. Today we live and serve by way of our gifts. Today we know it's in giving that we receive.

Principle- No one likes being "left behind".

Today is the first day of the rest of our lives!

<u>Creation</u>

YESTERDAY

Yesterday we didn't believe in God. We certainly didn't believe in Religion. Churches preached one message and demonstrated another. Evolution told us our distant cousins were snakes and piranhas. None of it made any practical sense.

We let go, focused on things we could change and served others

TODAY

Today, scientists worldwide agree, every human being is made up of their own proprietary DNA blueprint, consisting of over one million pages of highly organized & concise data in each of our 100 trillion+ cells. Today we know every blueprint requires a designer. Today we know blueprint complexity relates to designer complexity. Today we've reopened our hearts and minds to the possibility of an intelligent designer. Today we know we roll the dice but someone or something else determines how they land. Today we believe in a power greater than ourselves. (One gram of DNA can store 700 terabytes of data. That's 14,000 50-gigabyte Blu-ray discs…in a droplet of DNA that would fit on the tip of your pinky. To store the same kind of data on hard drives, the densest storage medium in use today, you'd need 233 3TB drives, weighing a total of *151 kilos*)

*Principle- Every blueprint requires a designer.

Today is the first day of the rest of our lives!

Daily Reflection

YESTERDAY

Yesterday life got on top of us. We could no longer manage the load. Feelings of hopelessness and despair eventually set in. We lost our faith. Many of us fell into addiction and depression. Without help we were in deep trouble.

We let go, focused on things we could change and served others

TODAY

Today we awake each day knowing our gifts and how to best live and serve by way of our gifts. Today we awake each day knowing exactly what we want, why we want it, and when we hope to achieve it by. Today we know thoughts become things. Today we know whatever we focus on we move towards. Today we awake to our goals. Today is the first day of the rest of our lives!

*Principle- Thoughts become things.

Today is the first day of the rest of our lives!

Delays vs. Denials

YESTERDAY

Yesterday we had places to go, people to see and deadlines that must be met. We had watches and we had calendars. Everything was on a manmade time schedule we had to follow. If we were told to plant a seed today, and make it sprout tomorrow, we forced our will on everyone if it meant getting that seed to sprout. Rational thought had left the building!

We let go, focus on things we can change and serve others

TODAY

Today we know God's delays are not God's denials. Today we know a seed grows on the creator's time clock...not ours! Today we roll the dice but certainly don't determine how they land. Today we accept life on life's terms. Today we have faith in a power greater than ourselves.

*Principle- Seeds grow on the creator's time clock...not ours!

Today is the first day of the rest of our lives!

<u>Depression</u>

YESTERDAY

Yesterday we focused on things we couldn't change over long periods of time. Fear, worry, guilt and shame created feelings of desperation and hopelessness. Fear led to anger. Anger led hate. Hate led to suffering. It was all about fear.

We let go, focused on things we could change and served others

TODAY

Today we know depression requires focus on self in order to exist. Today we know depression is pride in reverse. Today we know the moment we take focus off self and focus on serving others, depression dissolves. Today we focus on serving others. In today's world where almost 20,000 kid's die of starvation daily, we believe depression is a luxury...we have to have things pretty good to know how bad we have it!

*Principle- Depression requires focus on self in order to exist.

Today is the first day of the rest of our lives!

Disease of Entitlement

YESTERDAY

Yesterday drugs and entitlement were very similar in many ways. They were both highly addictive. We would stop at nothing to get what we wanted. We would do anything to get more. It was never enough. It always left us wanting more regardless of how much we had. It was an empty void that could never be filled. It destroyed key relationships.

* We've labelled entitlement as a disease in this book. We believe entitlement is the root cause of several mental illnesses and needs to be addressed.

We let go, focused on things we could change and served others

TODAY

Today we believe serving others is the only known cure for both addiction and entitlement. Today we're able to identify the disease of entitlement. Today we can separate those who need a hand up vs. a hand out. Today we're careful not to over water rootless grass (those living in entitlement).

*Principle- Today we're careful not to over water rootless grass.

Today is the first day of the rest of our lives!

<u>Disengage</u>

YESTERDAY

Yesterday we were "all in". There was little balance or moderation. We got caught up in other peoples stuff. We allowed third party problems to become ours. We let the wrong people in and couldn't get them out. We were unable to disengage.

We let go, focused on things we could change and served others

TODAY

Today we've learned to immediately disengage from things we can't change. Today we can stop, take a deep breath and refocus. Today we own our part in every situation. Today we know letting go of things we can't change is the secret to a happy, productive life. Today we know it only takes one sick person to destroy our lives. Today we know the only people we can change is ourselves.

*Principle- Letting go is a key to a happy life.

Today is the first day of the rest of our lives!

Dishonesty

YESTERDAY

Yesterday we were less than honest with ourselves and others. Over time, we believed our own press. Many of us who were incapable of getting honest lost their lives.

We let go, focused on things we could change and served others

TODAY

Today we know getting honest is the difference between life and death. Today we know rigorous self-honesty is our only chance! Today we've found the courage to let go, get honest and reach out to those we had harmed. Today we've found the courage to get honest with ourselves. Today we know courage is the only way to get honest and unlock the gift of humility. Today we know from the fountain of humility springs love, forgiveness, compassion and mercy. Today we know we can lie to others but we can't lie to ourselves. Today we lead with honesty and humility in everything we do.

*Principle- Getting honest is the difference between life and death.

Today is the first day of the rest of our lives!

Doctrine
"Fiction Packaged As Fact"

YESTERDAY

Yesterday our beliefs were based on doctrine we received from trusted sources; family, professionals, educators, ministries, media & government...and all in some pretty official terms! One day we opened our eyes and realized the information we received was biased fiction packaged as fact with a nice little bow...everyone had a motive!

We let go, focused on things we could change and served others

TODAY

Today we know the dietary food charts promoted by our trusted teachers for the past 50 years in our school systems were supplied by the industry selling the products. Today we know the medications promoted by our trusted doctors are supplied by the pharmaceutical companies. Today we know news provided by our trusted media is controlled and directed by select interest groups. Today we know doctrine and truth are not one in the same. Today we know, the disconnect felt between our fellow man, is the result of faulty doctrine. Today we've let go of the insanity, focus on things we can change and live and serve by way of our gifts. Today we put our faith in a power greater than ourselves.

*Principle- Fiction packaged as fact is still fiction.

Today is the first day of the rest of our lives!

<u>Doing What We Love</u>

YESTERDAY

Yesterday we were motivated by money. We never stopped to think we couldn't take any of it with us. We never stopped to think money might not bring happiness. We never stopped to think that money might be the root of our problems. Unfortunately chasing money cost most of us our happiness, our peace of mind, our freedom and in some cases our lives!

We let go, focused on things we could change and served others

TODAY

Today we've been introduced to our proprietary gifts. Today these gifts direct every area of our lives. Today we experience peace, joy and fulfilment like never before. Today we love what we do. Today we do what we love. Today we know living life and serving by way of our gifts is a key to a joyful life.

*Principle- Live and serve by way of our gifts.

Today is the first day of the rest of our lives!

Early Bird Gets the Worm

YESTERDAY

Yesterday we stayed up late. We woke up late. Typically nothing constructive happened after midnight. By the time we woke, those motivated had already accomplished half their objectives. Over time we were no longer on top of life...it was on top of us! Good things came to those who wait...but only what the hustlers had left behind!

We let go, focused on things we could change and served others

TODAY

Today we awake early. Today we start each day in gratitude and visualization. Today we know exactly what we want, why we want it and when we hope to achieve it by. Today we know starting each day early, with a clear focus, makes the difference between success and failure in almost every area of life. Today we focus on things we can change.

*Principle- The early bird gets the worm.

Today is the first day of the rest of our lives!

Eating an Elephant

YESTERDAY

Yesterday overwhelm was our #1 enemy. It drove us to highs, lows, addiction, depression, and everything in between. There was no moderation. Once we locked on, we couldn't disengage. Overwhelm drove many of us to premature death.

We let go, focused on things we could change and served others

TODAY

Today we know the only way to eat an elephant…one bite at a time! Today we take it easy, keep it simple, and stop and think before we act. Today we live in the moment, one day at a time. Today we know balance and moderation are keys to a happy, healthy life. Today we've learned to disengage and focus on things we can change.

*Principle- How do we eat an elephant… one bite at a time!

Today is the first day of the rest of our lives!

Encouragement

YESTERDAY

Yesterday we were surrounded by negativity. Negative people, discouraging words, unhealthy relationships...we were just hanging on! Discouraging words from close friends and family often took us down and kept us down. Overnight, we were single braided cords, walking alone without anyone to pick us up when we fell. Not a nice place to be!

We let go, focused on things we could change and served others

TODAY

Today we know any fool can condemn, criticize and complain and most fools do! Today we know the power of a few encouraging words. Today our mission is to encourage others to let go of the large burdens they carry. Today sharing a few words of encouragement with others is our greatest joy. Today we know life and death are in the power of the tongue. Today we share our experience, strength, and hope with others. Today we are strong triple braided cords no longer walking alone. Today we fellowship with likeminded people; serving by way of their gifts.

*Principle- Life and death are in the power of the tongue.

Today is the first day of the rest of our lives!

Fear

YESTERDAY

Yesterday stress, worry, frustration, and resentment were code names for fear. We were fearful of living and fearful of dying. We feared eating too much or not enough. We feared letting go and hanging on. Fear led to anger. Anger led to hate. Hate led to suffering. Fear was our #1 problem.

We let go, focused on things we could change and served others

TODAY

Today we know the moment we let go, and take focus off self, our fears disappear. Today we know everything decays, we're not here long and we can't take anything with us when we go. Today we believe in a power greater than ourselves. Today we know we can't be in fear and faith at the same time. Today we serve by way of our gifts. Today we accept life on life's terms. Today we live in peace.

*Principle- Can't be in fear and faith at the same time.

Today is the first day of the rest of our lives!

<u>Feeding the Bad Dog</u>

YESTERDAY

Yesterday negative energy, negative thoughts, negative influences and negative actions fed our bad dog. He grew bigger by the day. Before long, we couldn't control him. The bad dog had taken over. We were powerless.

We let go, focused on things we could change and served others

TODAY

Today we know a "good dog" and "bad dog" exist in each of us. Today we know the one we feed is the one that grows. Today we feed the "good dog" with an alkaline diet, positive thoughts, loving hearts, and an attitude of gratitude from the time we awake to the moment we sleep. Today we starve the "bad dog". Today we're very conscience of which dog we feed.

*Principle- The dog we feed is the dog that grows.

Today is the first day of the rest of our lives!

Fellowship

YESTERDAY

Yesterday we surrounded ourselves with the wrong people. We didn't realize it only took one bad apple to destroy an entire barrel of good ones. For many of us, we lay down with dogs and woke up with fleas. We had surrounded ourselves with selfish, self- centred takers, controllers and others whose primary focus was feeding the bad dog. For many, it cost us our lives.

We let go, focused on things we could change and served others

TODAY

Today we know spending time with happy, healthy, trustworthy friends is one of the greatest gifts we experience. Today we understand the importance of connecting with other likeminded individuals. Today we associate with givers and avoid takers knowing they end up hurting themselves and everyone around them in the process. Today we know it's better to walk our journey alone rather than let one dark person in. Today we know it only takes one dark person to take us down.

*Principle- It only takes one bad apple to destroy a barrel of good ones.

Today is the first day of the rest of our lives!

Focus

YESTERDAY

Yesterday our minds raced quickly. We couldn't get still. Our inability to focus created internal and external confusion. Lack of concentrated focus produced strong starters but weak finishers. We never completed anything we started. Our inability to focus left us feeling unworthy & struggling to fit in with others. When we did focus, we often focused on the wrong things.

We let go, focused on things we could change and served others

TODAY

Today we've gotten still. Today we keep our focus simple, measurable, and beneficial to all. Today we know whatever we focus on we move towards. Today we know obstacles are what we see when we take our eyes off our goals. Today we know what the mind can believe and the mind can conceive the mind can achieve. Today we focus on things we can change.

*Principle- What the mind can believe the mind can achieve.

Today is the first day of the rest of our lives!

Food

YESTERDAY

Yesterday we lived on acid. White sugar, white flour, white salt, processed foods, caffeine, alcohol, tobacco, narcotics...everything was acid! Stress and pressure created additional acid in the body. Our bodies and minds were toxic.

We let go, focused on things we could change and served others

TODAY

Today we know disease means dis-ease in the body. Today we know dis-ease comes from an abundance of acid. Today we've learned to eat and drink alkaline. Greens, water and lemon, watermelon, almonds and more greens! Today we avoid toxins at all costs. Today we know toxic foods create toxic thoughts which create toxic actions which create toxic habits which create toxic lives. Today we know toxins must be avoided at all costs.

*Principle- Healthier body makes for a healthier mind.

Today is the first day of the rest of our lives!

Forgiveness

YESTERDAY

Yesterday judgement and resentment went hand in hand. We judged others harshly. We resented almost everyone we came into contact with. Resentments were the #1 killer. Ironically, those we resented didn't even know we were resenting them. We suffered...not them!

We let go, focused on things we could change and served others

TODAY

Today we know resentments are nothing more than unrealistic expectations. Today we know resentments are like drinking poison and expecting the other person to die...it doesn't work! Today we know when one finger points out, three fingers point back. Today we're told even God doesn't judge people till their final day on earth...what gives us the right? Today we've learned to forgive ourselves and others. Today we live by a simple philosophy, judge not and ye shall not be judged. Today we accept life on life's terms. Today we've learned to love our enemies from afar.

*Principle- In order to forgive others, we must forgive ourselves first.

Today is the first day of the rest of our lives!

Givers vs. Takers

YESTERDAY

Yesterday we were selfish, self-centred takers. We entered relationships to get...not give! When we gave we gave to get. Giving to get wasn't giving! Sadly, we hurt ourselves and everyone around us in the process...our way didn't work! It was all about us!

We let go, focused on things we could change and served others

TODAY

Today we know every major religion worldwide tells a story of a giver and a taker. The giver is out to serve others and the taker is out to self-serve.
Today we choose to be givers; serving others by way of our gifts. Today we know takers hurt themselves and everyone around them in the process. Today we surround ourselves with givers and avoid takers at all cost. Today we know it only takes one taker to destroy our lives. Today we know it's in giving we receive. Today we know the only things we get to keep are the things we give away. Today we lead with love and encouragement. Today we lead by way of attraction...not promotion!

*Principle- Giving to get isn't giving...it's in giving that we receive.

Today is the first day of the rest of our lives!

Goals

YESTERDAY

Yesterday we had goals that had to be achieved at any and all costs. We did whatever we needed to do to get where we needed to go. It was all about us. For others, we no longer had goals. Our life had lost all meaning and purpose.

We let go, focused on things we could change and served others

TODAY

Today we have goals, meaning and purpose back in our lives. Today we've learned to focus on things we can change **without getting attached to the outcome**. Today we know what we want, why we want it and when we plan to achieve it by. Today we know obstacles are what we see when we take our eyes off our goals. Today we know God's delays are not God's denials. Today we know we roll the dice but certainly don't always determine how they land. Today we know there is a power greater than ourselves at work. Today we keep our goals simple, measurable and beneficial to all.

*Principle- Obstacles are what we see when we take our eyes off our goals.

Today is the first day of the rest of our lives!

God

YESTERDAY

Yesterday we didn't believe in God. We certainly didn't believe in Religion. Churches preached one message and demonstrated another. Evolution told us our distant cousins were snakes and piranhas. None of it made any practical sense.

We let go, focused on things we could change and served others

TODAY

Today we've reopened our hearts and minds to the idea of an intelligent designer. Today we know every living organism consists of its own unique proprietary blueprint. Today we know every blueprint requires a designer. Today we know scientists worldwide agree every human being is made up of their own proprietary DNA blueprint, consisting of over one million pages of highly organized data in each of our 100 trillion+ cells. Today we know we roll the dice but someone or something else determines how they land. Today we believe in a power greater than ourselves.

*Principle- A power greater than ourselves exists... absolutely!

Today is the first day of the rest of our lives!

Golden Rule

YESTERDAY

Yesterday, the golden rule was simple..."he with the gold made the rules!" Life was about trying to acquire as much gold as quickly as we could. Gold and profitability was often the only measuring stick. It was all about us.

We let go, focused on things we could change and served others

TODAY

Today we live by one golden rule...treat others the way we want to be treated! Today we focus on serving others by way of our gifts. Today we do unto others as we would have them do unto us. Today we know this one rule, if enforced, would change the world as we know it. Today it's in giving that we receive.

Principle- Treat others the way you want to be treated.

Today is the first day of the rest of our lives!

Gratitude

YESTERDAY

Yesterday we lived in expectation and entitlement. It was all about us. We always wanted more. It was never enough. We were always looking for something bigger and better. Habitually, we focused on what we didn't have. Our expectations were seldom met. More, more, more was our motto.

We let go, focused on things we could change and served others

TODAY

Today we start each day in gratitude; giving thanks for all the gifts we've been given. Today we know everything we have is a privilege...not a right! Today we focus on what we have vs. what we don't have. Today we know when we're grateful, we're rich! Today we know when we're grateful, we can't be fearful. Today we live with an attitude of gratitude. Today we know what's wrong is always available...and so is what's right!

*Principle- When we're grateful, we're rich.

Today is the first day of the rest of our lives!

<u>Half Pregnant</u>

YESTERDAY

Yesterday when it came to God, we were "half pregnant." We didn't believe in God until we were terminally ill or friends and family were sick and dying. We made promises to God in exchange for answered prayers. The moment our prayers were answered, we took our will back and started the process all over again. It was a viscous cycle. God was only called in for absolute emergencies..."God Help Us"! Once again...it was all about us!

We let go, focused on things we could change and served others

TODAY

Today we let go absolutely knowing our way didn't work and half measures availed us nothing. Today we know we have to have the courage to take our foot off first base if we ever want to get to second. Today we've surrendered our will knowing we can roll the dice but someone or something else determines how they land. Today we ask how we may best serve by way of our gifts. Today we know religions worldwide preach the same message..."surrender your will or perish"! Today we believe in a power greater than ourselves.

*Principle- No such thing as half pregnant...we must let go absolutely!

Today is the first day of the rest of our lives!

Hard Wiring

YESTERDAY

Yesterday we struggled through life unaware of our talents and gifts. Most of us had never heard of spiritual gifts. Forcing our will and forging our path was all we knew. We were always pushing!

We let go, focused on things we could change and served others

TODAY

Today we've learned our unique gifts. Today we apply those gifts in every area of our lives. Today when we live by way of our gifts we're being pulled...we're not pushing! Today we teach others how to apply their gifts so they in turn can teach others. Today we know we're all hard wired with different gifts. Today we experience peace and joy like never before.

*Principle- When we live by way of our gifts we're being pulled...not pushing.

Today is the first day of the rest of our lives!

Head vs. Heart

YESTERDAY

Yesterday our heads and hearts were disconnected. Our minds told us one thing...our hearts another! Our beliefs and our behaviours often ran counter to one another. When our hearts and heads weren't aligned we lived in torment.

We let go, focused on things we could change and served others

TODAY

Today we've learned our gifts. Today we apply those gifts in every area of our lives. Today, living by way of our gifts aligns our heads and our hearts. Today we know when our heads and hearts align we have peace. Today we know learning our gifts is the secret to a happy life.

Principle- When our heads and hearts align, we experience peace.

Today is the first day of the rest of our lives!

Helping Others

YESTERDAY

Yesterday we were selfish and self-centred. It was all about us. Our hearts and minds were closed to the thought of helping others. When we gave, we gave to get! Ego, will, pride and greed drove us to self-service at all cost. If nothing else we were consistent!

We let go, focused on things we could change and served others

TODAY

Today we've learned to smash our ego; knowing our way didn't work. Today we work on deflating self and inflating and encouraging others. Today we live by a motto "help each other don't hurt each other". Today we wake up to give...not to get! Today we know it's in giving that we receive. Today we know we can't take anything with us when we go. Today we know the only things we get to keep are the things we give away. Today we lead with love and encouragement.

*Principle- Help each other...don't hurt each other".

Today is the first day of the rest of our lives!

Humility

YESTERDAY

Yesterday we were incapable of getting honest with ourselves. Without honesty, there was no humility. Without honesty, there was no chance! We told people what we wanted them to hear. We showed people what we wanted them to see. We told ourselves the same story so long that we started believing our own press. We hung on to our old beliefs. We forced our will on others. We were afraid to let go.

We let go, focused on things we could change and served others

TODAY

Today we know courage is a key to self-honesty. Today we know self-honesty is the secret to humility. From a foundation of humility grows love, forgiveness, acceptance and gratitude. Today we're able to take a fearless moral inventory of ourselves and forgive both ourselves and others. Today we've reached out to those we had harmed and let them know we are sorry. Today we live with an open heart and open mind. Today we no longer force our will on anyone. Today we know we roll the dice but certainly don't determine how they land. Today we believe in a power greater than ourselves. Today we accept life on life's terms.

Principle- Courage is a key to self-honesty...honesty leads to humility.

Today is the first day of the rest of our lives!

It's Not the Load

YESTERDAY

Yesterday overwhelm was our greatest enemy. Once overwhelmed; rational thought quickly dissipated. Once irrational; anything and everything became possible. Insanity best described many of our actions. We became unmanageable, ultimately collapsing under our own loads.

We let go, focused on things we could change and served others

TODAY

Today we know; it's not the load it's how we carry it! Today we know there is only one way to eat an elephant...one bite at a time! Today we focus on things we can change, not things we can't. Today we no longer get attached to the outcome knowing we roll the dice but certainly don't determine how they land. Today we no longer try to change others; we know the only people we can change is ourselves. Today we've learned to accept life on life's terms. Today we no longer own other people's stuff. Today we live one day at a time, knowing tomorrow isn't promised to anyone.

*Principle- It's not the load; it's how we carry it.

Today is the first day of the rest of our lives!

Judging Others

YESTERDAY

Yesterday we judged others harshly. We showed little patience or tolerance. We held grudges. We were slow to forgive and quick to anger. Our need to maintain control was paramount. If people didn't do what we wanted, when we wanted or how we wanted, we had no use for them. It was our way or no way!

We let go, focused on things we could change and served others

TODAY

Today we know any fool can condemn, criticize and complain and most fools do! Today we've learned when one finger points out, three fingers point back. Today we're told even God doesn't judge people until their last day here on earth...what gives us the right! Today we've learned to accept life on life's terms. Today we practice "judge not and ye shall not be judged". Today we come from a place of love and encouragement. Today we believe in a power greater than ourselves. Today we've learned to love our enemies from afar. Today we know the only people we can change is ourselves.

*Principle- Judge not and ye shall not be judged.

Today is the first day of the rest of our lives!

KISS Principle

YESTERDAY

Yesterday we carried a big load. Life was complicated. If it wasn't, we made it complicated. We owned other people's stuff. We took other people's inventory. We constantly focused on things we couldn't change. In many cases, we enjoyed levels of pressure and chaos. Ultimately overwhelm was our greatest enemy.

We let go, focused on things we could change and served others

TODAY

Today we live by way of the KISS principle (keep it simple stupid). Today we've let go of the things we can't change. Today we start each day in gratitude knowing when we're grateful we're rich. Today we know what we want, why we want it and when we hope to achieve it by. Today we live and serve by way of our gifts. Today we know the only people we can change is ourselves. Today we know we can roll the dice but we don't determine how they land. Today we know every moment is a gift...not a right! Today we keep it simple!

*Principle-KISS- Keep it simple stupid.

Today is the first day of the rest of our lives!

Laughter

YESTERDAY

Yesterday life was complicated. Pressure, responsibilities, stress, and deadlines that must be met. Life had become a pressure cooker. Jokes were for kids. We had no time to joke around. After all there was little to no value in laughter. Time was short and we had objectives that must be met.

We let go, focused on things we could change and served others

TODAY

Today we know laughter heals sickness. Today we know laughter lightens the heaviest of loads. Today we know nothing in life ever happens so bad we can't either laugh at it or learn something from it. Today we know laughter is one of many secrets to a happy, healthy life. Today we keep joke books close by!

*Principle- Laughter heals sickness.

Today is the first day of the rest of our lives!

Leadership

YESTERDAY

Yesterday we put our faith in family, friends and trusted partners. We trusted our governments, mainstream media, medical doctors, church leaders, etc. One day we realized our trust had been breached on almost every front. Our faith in mankind had let us down. Sadly most of our trusted leaders were takers with an agenda and little to no consequence for their actions. Our leaders were there to self-serve...not serve others!

We let go, focused on things we could change and served others

TODAY

Today every animal on planet earth continues to survive without the leadership of mankind. Today the sun continues to rise and set without the leadership of mankind. Today we see the leadership of mankind driving animals into extinction faster than ever before. Today we know everything we needed to survive from fruits, nuts, vegetables and fresh water were here from day 1...before the leadership of mankind! Today we know we roll the dice but someone or something else determine how they land. Today we know we're powerless over our birth, our death and most things in between. Today we believe in a power greater than ourselves. Today we awake each morning asking how we may best serve. Today we live and serve by way of our gifts.

*Principle- We roll the dice but someone or something else determines how they land.

Today is the first day of the rest of our lives!

Leading By Example

YESTERDAY

Yesterday we preached one message and demonstrated another. Our thoughts and actions were consistently self-serving. We expected others to do as we said, not as we did! We led by way of manipulation, fear and control. It was all about us.

We let go, focused on things we could change and served others

TODAY

Today we live by a motto, "help each other don't hurt each other". Today we follow one golden rule "treat others the way we want to be treated". Today we lead by way of attraction, not promotion. Today we lead by example. Today we put principles before personalities. Today we lead with honesty, humility, love and acceptance. Today we lead with love and encouragement. Today we live and serve by way of our gifts.

*Principle- Always lead by example.

Today is the first day of the rest of our lives!

Letting Go...Absolutely

YESTERDAY

Yesterday we refused to let go of the past. We carried guilt, shame, anger and resentment. We constantly lived in torment. Focusing on things we couldn't change over long periods of time led to mental illness and often premature death. The thought of letting go was terrifying. There was no one left in the theatre but we couldn't stop performing! We simply couldn't let go!

We let go, focused on things we could change and served others

TODAY

Today we know our old ways didn't work...we proved it! Today we found the courage to let go absolutely knowing half measures availed us nothing. Today we've learned to forgive ourselves and others knowing that we all make mistakes. Today we've cleared away the wreckage of our past by reaching out to those we had harmed and made amends to them all. Today we started over as the first day of the rest of our lives. Today we know life is short, life is difficult and we can't take anything with us. Today we know, we can't change the past, we can't guarantee the future and this moment is all that we have. Today we know the past doesn't have to equal the future unless we let it.

*Principle- Half measures availed us nothing...we must let go absolutely. We can't be half pregnant!

Today is the first day of the rest of our lives!

Life Is Difficult

YESTERDAY

Yesterday no one told us life was difficult. We were taught we could have whatever we wanted if we worked hard enough! We had rights. We had expectations. We had privileges. We had entitlements.

We let go, focused on things we could change and served others

TODAY

Today we know almost 20,000 children die of starvation daily. Today we know 1 in 5 no longer have fresh drinking water. Today we know pain and suffering now surround us worldwide. Today we know every moment free of pain and suffering is a precious gift. Today we know everything we have, right down to the shoes on our feet, is a privilege...not a right! Today we live in gratitude for all that we have. Today we focus on the top 10% of life...not the bottom 10%! Today we focus on serving others while we can, knowing life is short, life is difficult and we can't take anything with us when we go. As a wise comedian once said..."life sucks...wear a helmet!"

*Principle- Life is difficult... as soon as we realize this every moment free of pain and suffering is a precious gift!

Today is the first day of the rest of our lives!

<u>Listening</u>

YESTERDAY

Yesterday our minds and hearts were closed. We only listened if and when it benefitted us. For many our minds raced...we couldn't get still. For others we were too busy scheming and calculating. Listening and caring went hand in hand. Unfortunately most of us didn't care about anyone other than ourselves.

We let go, focused on things we could change and served others

TODAY

Today we know listening and caring go hand in hand. Today we know "no one cares how much we know until they know how much we care". Today we've learned to quiet our minds through mediation and prayer. Today we've learned to reopen our heart and minds. Today we're open and willing to listen. Today we know listening is a key to serving others. Today we understand we're given two ears and one mouth so we listen twice as much as we talk.

*Principle- No one cares how much we know until they know how much we care.

Today is the first day of the rest of our lives!

Living in the Moment

YESTERDAY

Yesterday we drove 100 mph looking in the rear view mirror and couldn't understand why our lives were one accident after another. Moving forward and looking into the past was a recipe for disaster. If we weren't living in the past we were always planning our future. Either way, we were missing the biggest gift life had to offer...the present!

We let go, focused on things we could change and served others

TODAY

Today we know we can't change the past, we can't guarantee the future and today is the first day of the rest of our lives. Today we live just for today. Today we've learned to accept life on life's terms. Today we know we roll the dice but whatever comes of today is often beyond our control. Today we know the future isn't promised to anyone. Today we know life is short, life is difficult and we can't take anything with us. Today we know each moment is a gift and a privilege...not a right!

*Principle- This moment is a gift...that's why they call it "present".

Today is the first day of the rest of our lives!

Living Life to the Fullest

YESTERDAY

Yesterday we lived in fear. Fear of loss. Fear of success. Our hearts and minds were closed. We were constantly distracted. We focused on things we couldn't change. As the world passed us by with infinite gifts; we were busy fighting over the table scraps.

We let go, focused on things we could change and served others

TODAY

Today we've let go of the things we can't change. Today we've reopened our hearts and minds to the infinite possibilities. Today we awake each morning in gratitude for all the precious gifts we've been given. Today we've learned our gifts and how to best direct them. Today we know what we want, why we want it and when we want it by. Today we experience peace, joy, love, compassion, humility...it's a miracle! Today we know it's not only about the length of our lives...it's about the width! Today we live...not prepare to live!

Principle- The width of one's life is as important as the length!

Today is the first day of the rest of our lives!

Love

YESTERDAY

Yesterday we entered relationships to get love...not give it! Turned out love with conditions wasn't love at all...it was control! The moment we didn't get our way, the love affair was over. We jumped from one relationship to another seeking fulfilment. We were seeking love externally. How could we give what we didn't have? How could we love another if we never loved ourselves?

We let go, focused on things we could change and served others

TODAY

Today we know relationships are a place we go to give love...not get it! Today we know love starts with the internal before we can love externally. Today we've learned to love ourselves and others. Today we understand the power of unconditional love and forgiveness. Today we know true love conquers all.

*Principle- Love with conditions is control.

Today is the first day of the rest of our lives!

<u>Love Thy Enemy</u>

YESTERDAY

Yesterday we despised our enemy. Love was the last thing on our mind when it came to our enemies. Ironically our hate, anger, negativity, resentments and hardship fed our bad dog...not our enemies! It was like drinking poison and expecting our enemies to die...total insanity!

We let go, focused on things we could change and served others

TODAY

Today we've let go and owned up to our part in every situation. Today we've reached out to those we had harmed and made amends to them all. Today we understand our enemies are often our greatest teachers. Today we've learned to love our enemies even if we have to love them from afar. Today we've come to understand the true power of unconditional love.

*Principle- Our enemies are often our greatest teachers.

Today is the first day of the rest of our lives!

<u>Lying To Ourselves</u>

YESTERDAY

Yesterday we told ourselves story after story. We reasoned, rationalized, and justified. Eventually we started believing our own press. We kept ourselves distracted from reality. We lied to others but couldn't lie to ourselves. Over time lying got easier. Eventually no one trusted us...not even ourselves!

We let go, focused on things we could change and served others

TODAY

Today we've found the courage to get honest...rigorously honest! This was the one step we had to get right or our chances were zero! Through self-honesty came the gift of humility. It was only through humility could we find true love, forgiveness, compassion and the gift of mercy. Today we've reached out to those we had harmed and made amends to them all. Today we live by way of our gifts. Today when we're wrong we promptly admit it. Today we keep an open heart and open mind on all subjects towards all people. Today we accept life on life's terms. Today we know we can always lie to other people but we can't lie to ourselves.

*Principle- We can lie to others but we can't lie to ourselves.

Today is the first day of the rest of our lives!

Manipulation

YESTERDAY

Yesterday we tried changing and manipulating others to get what we wanted...nothing complicated here! We had objectives that had to be met. We required others to help us achieve our goals. For many we would stop at nothing if it benefitted us. Lying, deceiving and manipulating were some of the tools. We were very sick.

We let go, focused on things we could change and served others

TODAY

Today we focus on giving vs. taking. Today we ask how we may serve others by way of our gifts. Today we lead with love and encouragement. Today we no longer force our will on others. Today we accept life on life's terms. Today we know we roll the dice but don't control how they land. Today we live in gratitude rather than expectation and entitlement. Today we're no longer attached to the outcome. Today we know the only people we can change is ourselves.

*Principle- Givers encourage...takers manipulate.

Today is the first day of the rest of our lives!

Meditation and Prayer

YESTERDAY

Yesterday meditation and prayer were religious words. We wanted nothing to do with either. We had trust issues surrounding church and religion. People who preached one message and demonstrated another were considered dishonest or hypocritical. We had experienced enough religion to last us a lifetime.

We let go, focused on things we could change and served others

TODAY

Today we see signs of an intelligent designer in everything; from a seed, to a hummingbird, to a tree that exhales our fresh oxygen and inhales our poisonous carbon dioxide. Today we quiet our minds by way of meditation and prayer. Today we believe inspiration comes from the art of getting still. Today we get still and listen. Today we know the greatest prayer we can give is...thank you!

*Principle- Getting still is key to receiving inspiration.

Today is the first day of the rest of our lives!

Mentors

YESTERDAY

Yesterday we let the wrong people in. Once in they were difficult to get out. Soon negative takers surrounded us. Before long we became one! Our thoughts and actions became dark. We crossed lines we never thought we would cross. For many of us it took only one bad influence to destroy our entire lives.

We let go, focused on things we could change and served others

TODAY

Today we walk alone rather than let the wrong people in. Today we know it only takes one bad influence to destroy our lives. Today we surround ourselves with likeminded givers who focus on serving others by way of their gifts. Today our mentors lead with love, compassion, wisdom and patience. Today we serve others by way of our gifts and encourage them to serve others by way of their gifts. Today we know yesterday's liabilities are our greatest assets when mentoring others.

*Principle- Be the change we wish to see in this world.

Today is the first day of the rest of our lives!

Miracles

YESTERDAY

Yesterday it was never enough. We always wanted more. Regardless of the gifts we were given we needed more. Habitually we focused on the bottom 10% while the top 10% simply passed us by! We were locked in expectation and entitlement.

We let go, focused on things we could change and served others

TODAY

Today we see miracles surrounding us everywhere. Today we know our hearts have beaten without a break from the moment we were born. Today we know trees inhale the poisonous carbon dioxide we exhale and exhale "life" in the form of the oxygen we inhale. Today we know the precise proximity of the sun keeps us from freezing or burning up. Today we see miracles around us every moment. Today we know everything we've been given is a precious gift and a privilege...not a right! Today we live in gratitude...not entitlement. Today we've reopened our hearts and our minds to the possibility of an intelligent designer.

*Principle- We are powerless over our birth, our death, and most things in between.

Today is the first day of the rest of our lives!

Motto to Live By

YESTERDAY

Yesterday it was all about us. We were takers...nothing complicated here! We did what we wanted, when we wanted, how we wanted. Our motto was more, more, more...it was never enough! If we had to hurt those around us in the process, it was a cost of doing business. We were greedy, selfish and self-centred.

We let go, focused on things we could change and served others

TODAY

Today we live by a simple motto..."help each other, don't hurt each other". Today we share this motto with those we let in close. When those closest to us consistently breach this motto, we simply have to love them from afar. Today we treat others the way we want to be treated. Today we focus on serving others...not self-serving!

*Principle- Help each other, don't hurt each other.

Today is the first day of the rest of our lives!

Nature

YESTERDAY

Yesterday we spent most of our time in a box house, box car, box office or staring into a box screen watching movies, playing games, working etc. We completely lost touch with nature, our creator and the miracles that exist around us. We were moving so fast we never took the time to slow down. We were distracted to the point that everything real had lost its meaning.

We let go, focused on things we could change and served others

TODAY

Today we know the answer to all life's questions exist in nature. Today we get outside, breathe, get still and witness the miracles all around us. Today we know a still mind opens the door to inspiration. Today we spend as much time in the outdoors and nature as we can. Today we know a healthy body and healthy mind are connected. Today we notice God's little miracles surrounding us while in nature.

*Principle- All the answers to life's problems can be found in nature.

Today is the first day of the rest of our lives!

<u>Negativity</u>

YESTERDAY

Yesterday negativity surrounded us. News, media, television, movies, internet, video games, family, friends, coworkers...negative influences were everywhere! Over time our thoughts, actions, habits and speech grew dark. We started focusing on the bottom 10% in every situation. We criticized, condemned and complained. We grew angry, resentful and often hateful. We had no idea how we got here or how to get out...we were stuck!

We let go, focused on things we could change and served others

TODAY

Today we've simply let go and started today as the first day of the rest of our lives. Today we've learned our gifts and how to best serve ourselves and others by way of our gifts. Today we start each day in gratitude for all that we're grateful for. Today we have a new vision, a new plan and a new strategy to carry out that plan. Today we've surrounded ourselves with good people or we walk our journey alone. Today we know it only takes one bad person to destroy our lives. Today we know a positive mental attitude is the difference between success and failure. Today we focus on the top 10% of every situation...not the bottom 10%. Today we feed the good dog!

*Principle- Focus on the top 10%...not the bottom 10%.

Today is the first day of the rest of our lives!

<u>Obstacles</u>

YESTERDAY

Yesterday we focused on things we couldn't change over long periods of time. Whatever we focused on, we moved towards. The more obstacles we focused on, the more appeared. Personal failure became a self-fulfilling prophecy. We were stuck.

We let go, focused on things we could change and served others

TODAY

Today we know obstacles are what we see when we take our eyes off our goals. Today we've let go of the things we can't change and focus on the things we can change. Today we know thoughts become things. Today we know what we want, why we want it and when we want it by. Today we have a vision and a plan to carry it out! Today we know what's wrong is always available...but so is what's right.

Principle- Obstacles are what we see when we take our eyes off your goals.

Today is the first day of the rest of our lives!

Page 69

Open Mindedness

YESTERDAY

Yesterday our hearts and our minds were closed. We weren't willing to learn anything new unless it benefitted us directly. We were often too busy calculating or forcing our will on others. It was our way or no way. Sadly our ways didn't work but we refused to let go as a matter a pride.

We let go, focused on things we could change and served others

TODAY

Today we've reopened our hearts and minds like little children. Today we keep an open mind on all subjects towards all people. Today we come from a place of love and encouragement. Today we come from a place of acceptance and humility. Today we get still and listen. Today we no longer force our will on others. Today we've opened our hearts and minds to the idea of an intelligent designer. Today we know we roll the dice but certainly don't determine how they land. Today we believe in a power greater than ourselves.

*Principle-Today we keep an open heart and mind.

Today is the first day of the rest of our lives!

<u>Ownership</u>

YESTERDAY

Yesterday it was all about acquiring "stuff". The more we had the better off we were. Need for ownership was paramount. It was never enough. Putting finance before all else cost us more than we bargained for. We carried the weight of the world on our shoulders trying to acquire and maintain. Eventually we collapsed under our own load. It was simply too much to bear.

We let go, focused on things we could change and served others

TODAY

Today we know life is short, life is difficult and we can't take anything with us when we go. Today we know everything decays. Today we know the only things we get to keep are the things we give away. Today we know it's in giving that we receive. Today we know the best things in life are free. Today we focus on serving others by way of the gifts we've been so graciously given. Today we know every novelty has an expiry date.

*Principle-Every novelty has an expiry date.

Today is the first day of the rest of our lives!

<u>Owning Our Part</u>

YESTERDAY

Yesterday it was never our fault. We redirected blame in any direction if it meant saving ourselves. We became experts at taking other peoples inventory. As long as we focused on other people's stuff we never had to look at our own!

We let go, focused on things we could change and served others

TODAY

Today we know in order to let go we first have to own up to it! Today we know once we get honest, and own up to it, we get to let it go, **forever**, and start today as the first day of the rest of our lives. Today we've taken a searching and fearless moral inventory of ourselves. Today we've reached out and made amends to those we had harmed. Today we've cleared away the wreckage of our past. Today we're the first to admit when we're wrong. Yesterday's liabilities are today's greatest assets when serving others!

*Principle-We must own up to it first...only then can we let go of it!

Today is the first day of the rest of our lives!

Passion vs. Desire

YESTERDAY

Yesterday we forced our wills on others if it meant getting what we wanted, when we wanted, how we wanted. Our wants and desires were often met at any cost. Self-will had run riot.

We let go, focused on things we could change and served others

TODAY

Today we know passions pull us and desires require us to push. Today we no longer push. Today we no longer force our will on others. Today we've tapped into our passions by learning our spiritual gifts. Today we live and serve by way of our passions and gifts. Today we live with passion.

*Principle-Passions pull us...desires require we push!

Today is the first day of the rest of our lives!

Past Does Not Equal the Future

YESTERDAY

We had lost in business. We had lost in love. We had lost key friendships. It was too late for us. Our destiny was predetermined...a self-fulfilling prophecy!

We let go, focused on things we could change and served others

TODAY

Today we know the past does not equal the future unless we let it. Today we've started over as the first day of the rest of our lives. Today we've learned our unique gifts and talents. Today we know what we want, why we want it and when we hope to achieve it by. Today we've let go of the people, places and things that once held us down. Today we know whatever we focus on we move towards. Today we focus up to 90% of our thoughts and actions on things we can change vs. things we can't!

*Principle-Past doesn't equal the future...unless we let it!

Today is the first day of the rest of our lives!

<u>Patience</u>

YESTERDAY

Yesterday we had very little patience. Instant gratification drove us to obsessive compulsive disorders such as overeating, drug and alcohol abuse and often much worse. Our expectations and entitlements drove us to selfish, self-centred behaviours.

We let go, focused on things we could change and served others

TODAY

Today we know seeds grow on God's time clock...not ours! Today we've learned to accept life on life's terms. Today we know the only people we can change is ourselves. Today we've learned to accept people, places and things as they are. Today we know we may roll the dice but someone or something else determines how they land. Today we know everything has a season. Today we know patience, wisdom and genius are often one in the same. Today we believe in a power greater than ourselves.

*Principle-Patience, genius and wisdom are often one in the same.

Today is the first day of the rest of our lives!

<u>Paying It Forward</u>

YESTERDAY

Yesterday we were selfish and self-centred. It was all about us. When we gave we gave to get. Sadly self-serving hurt everyone including ourselves.

We let go, focused on things we could change and served others

TODAY

Today we know focus on self is the root cause of depression, anxiety, addiction, grandiosity, codependency and many other illnesses. Today we've taken focus off self and focus on serving others. Today we live and serve others by way of the unique gifts we've been freely given. Today we know it's in giving we receive. Today we know the only things we get to keep are the things we give away. Today we enjoy giving as much as getting. Today we take the precious gifts we've been so graciously given and pay it forward. Today we teach others to teach others to teach others!

*Principle- Focus on self is the root cause of addiction, depression, codependency and many other mental illnesses.

Today is the first day of the rest of our lives!

Peer Pressure

YESTERDAY

We associated with the wrong people...nothing complicated here! Once inside we allowed ourselves to be directed, controlled and influenced. Third party expectations were soon placed on us. We were pressured into doing things we knew were wrong. We felt we had no choice. Poor choices in friends cost many of us our lives.

We let go, focused on things we could change and served others

TODAY

Today we've been given a second chance. Today we walk with healthy, likeminded individuals or we walk our journey alone. Today we know the only people we can change is ourselves. Today we no longer allow ourselves to be negatively influenced. Today we no longer own other people's stuff! Today we've learned to disengage from third party problems. Today we've learned to love our enemies from afar. Today we focus on giving and associate with givers. Today we avoid taking and takers knowing it only takes one rotten apple to destroy an entire barrel.

*Principle- Only takes one rotten apple to destroy an entire barrel.

Today is the first day of the rest of our lives!

<u>Perceptions</u>

YESTERDAY

Yesterday perceptions and reality were one in the same. We assumed everyone's perceptions matched our own. When our perceptions were threatened we felt violated. We stopped at nothing to defend our perceptions.

We let go, focused on things we could change and served others

TODAY

Today we know perceptions and reality are not one in the same. Today we know perceptions are nothing more than personal opinions based on past experiences. Today we've reopened our hearts and minds. Today we no longer force our perceptions on others. Today we're able to love, encourage and accept others regardless of their perceptions. Today we fellowship with likeminded individuals. Today we've learned its okay to love others from afar.

*Principle- Perception and reality are not one in the same.

Today is the first day of the rest of our lives!

Pets

YESTERDAY

Yesterday we sought after unconditional love our entire lives. Friends, family members, partners, marriages, churches...where was the unconditional love? Love with conditions was nothing more than control. New relationships were nothing more than a novelty with an expiry date. Our trust had been breached on almost every front. We were damaged.

We let go, focused on things we could change and served others

TODAY

Today we feel a sense of unconditional love and loyalty from our pets....especially dogs! They love us. They serve us. They're loyal to us. They trust us. They show us affection, compassion and respect. Our pets fill us with love. Today we know pets are a source of love. Today we know we're able to pass on the love we get from our pets to others.

*Principle- Pets are a great source of love.

Today is the first day of the rest of our lives!

Positive Affirmations

YESTERDAY

Yesterday negativity surrounded us! Sarcasm was considered funny. Disrespect was considered cool. Condemning, criticizing and complaining were openly accepted. Television, video games, internet, music...negativity was often the focus. Negative thoughts, negative actions and negative habits often led to torment and misery. Only in a world gone completely mad could some of these things seem normal!

We let go, focused on things we could change and served others

TODAY

Today we start each day with positive comments and statements which create positive thoughts, positive actions, healthy habits and healthy and happy lives. Today we repeat the same phrases over and over to reinforce our beliefs and our behaviours. Today we say things like; "today is going to be the best day of my life." Today we start each and every day with positive affirmations.

*Principle- Today we start each day with positive affirmations.

Today is the first day of the rest of our lives!

Positive Mental Attitude

YESTERDAY

Yesterday negativity surrounded us. Negative people, negative energy, negativity via television, video games, internet...we couldn't escape it! In math we learned a simple principle...a negative plus a negative was a larger negative! The more negativity surrounding us the worse off we were...nothing complicated here!

We let go, focused on things we could change and served others

TODAY

Today we're surrounded by positive people or we walk our journey alone. Today we associate with givers...not takers. Today we understand the principle of negativity. Today we know that one bad apple will destroy an entire barrel of good apples. Today we focus on the top 10% in every situation... not the bottom 10%. Today we constantly ask ourselves...what can we learn from this? Today we know according to Napoleon Hill's bestselling book of the last century, "Think and Grow Rich", a positive mental attitude is the #1 common denominator among the world's most successful people.

*Principle- Positive mental attitude is the #1 common denominator among the world's most successful people.

Today is the first day of the rest of our lives!

Power of a Smile

YESTERDAY

Yesterday we lived in anger, resentment, disappointment, stress and fear. We were hurt, distrusting and often hateful. We had nothing to be happy about. The last thing on our mind was smiling or being grateful.

We let go, focused on things we could change and served others

TODAY

Today we know a smile lights up the darkest of rooms. Today we know the power of a smile is one of the greatest gifts on earth. Today we know living and serving by way of our gifts brings a level of joy and happiness we've never experienced. Today we know smiling and laughter heals sickness. Today we know what's wrong is always available...but so is what's right! Today we know when we're grateful...we're rich! Today we keep a joke book close by.

*Principle- Smiles and laughter heal sickness.

Today is the first day of the rest of our lives!

Power of Habits

YESTERDAY

Yesterday habits were nothing more than actions without thought. For some it was coffee, cigarettes, cola, white sugar, white salt, alcohol & drugs. For others it was walking, reading, serving, loving, accepting, caring & sharing. Our habits created our character. We were the result of our daily actions...nothing complicated here!

We let go, focused on things we could change and served others

TODAY

Today we understand our thoughts direct our actions which create the habits that create our character. Today we understand habits are nothing more than actions without thought. Today we've let go of our old habits and started again with new thoughts and actions. Today we chose life over death. Today we know when we put healthy things into our minds, bodies and spirits, healthy stuff eventually has to come out! Today our choices and habits are simple, healthy and service orientated.

*Principle- Habits are actions without thought.

Today is the first day of the rest of our lives!

<u>Prayer</u>

YESTERDAY

Yesterday prayer was religious terminology...certainly not for us! If we were in serious trouble and had no other choice but to look to our higher power....maybe! We had little to no faith in man's spin on God or Religion.

We let go, focused on things we could change and served others

TODAY

Today we know we roll the dice but someone or something else determines how they land. Today we've reopened our minds, hearts and eyes to the intelligent design surrounding us in everything; from a butterfly, to a rainbow, to a newborn baby. Today we get still and give thanks for all that we have. Today we know everything we've been given is a privilege...not a right! Today we've come to believe in a power greater than ourselves.

*Principle- Greatest prayer in life is...thank you!

Today is the first day of the rest of our lives!

Pride

YESTERDAY

Yesterday pride in forward gear was grandiosity and pride in reverse was depression...they both required focus on self! Pride was considered the deadliest of the seven sins and the source of all others. Sin was identified as; a desire to be more important or attractive than others, failing to acknowledge the good work of others, and excessive love of self. Yesterday we lived in expectation and entitlement. It was all about us.

We let go, focused on things we could change and served others

TODAY

Today we know the moment we take focus off self, grandiosity and depression quickly dissipate. Today we know almost every religion worldwide teaches the same message..."surrender your will or perish"! Today we've let go and live, love and serve others by way of our gifts. Today we've let go of ego, will, pride and greed and reset today as the first day of the rest of our lives. Today we know it's in giving that we truly receive.

*Principle- Pride in forward gear is grandiosity and pride in reverse is depression...they both required focus on self!

Today is the first day of the rest of our lives!

Principles before Personalities

YESTERDAY

Yesterday we associated with those we best related to. Unfortunately we were selfish, self-centred takers with one measurable objective...self-gratification! The path of self-gratification cost many of us our lives.

We let go, focused on things we could change and served others

TODAY

Today we live by principles. Today we associate with givers...not takers. Today we focus on serving others...not self-serving! Today we treat others the way we want to be treated. Today we help one another, not hurt one another. Today we come from a place of honesty, humility, acceptance and gratitude. Today we no longer force our will on others. Today we keep an open mind and open heart, on all subjects, with all people. Today we know the only people we can change is ourselves. Today we've learned to love our enemies from afar. Today we place principles before personalities.

*Principle- Today we place principles before personalities.

Today is the first day of the rest of our lives!

Proactive vs. Reactive

YESTERDAY

Yesterday we allowed others to direct us, control us and influence us. We allowed outside influences to upset our internal balance and harmony. We were often victimized by conditions surrounding us. Overwhelm often created electrical storms in our minds. Once in overwhelm we couldn't think clearly. Irrational thoughts created irrational decisions. Before long we were buried!

We let go, focused on things we could change and served others

TODAY

Today we've simply let go of the thing we can't change and focus on the things we can change. Today we know obstacles are what we see when we take our eyes off our goals. Today we keep our eyes on our goals. Today we know the only people we can change is ourselves. Today we know what we want, why we want it and when we hope to achieve it by.

*Principle- Direct your own destiny before someone else does it for you.

Today is the first day of the rest of our lives!

Problems

YESTERDAY

Yesterday we focused on things we couldn't change. Yesterday we focused on the bottom 10% of most situations. Yesterday we thrived on negativity. Yesterday obstacles surrounded us as we had no goals.

We let go, focused on things we could change and served others

TODAY

Today we focus on things we can change. Today we know obstacles are what we see when we take our eyes off our goals. Today we know what's wrong is always available...but so is what's right! Today we know it's not the load...it's how we carry the load. Today we know there are few lessons in success. Today we focus on the top 10%...not the bottom 10%. Today we know problems are a sign of life. Today we know the only people without problems are those living in graveyards. Today with every problem we ask ourselves two questions; **can we change it? and what can we learn from it?** Today we accept life on life on life's terms.

*Principle-What's wrong is always available...but so is what's right.

Today is the first day of the rest of our lives!

Procrastination

YESTERDAY

Yesterday we put everything off until tomorrow, next week or next year. We told ourselves story after story, rationalized and justified. Failing to take action cost us everything. Over time motivation, determination and focus slowly dissipated. One day slowly rolled into another...we were stuck! Procrastination was a silent killer.

TODAY

We let go, focused on things we could change and served others

Today we know life is short...we're not here long! Today we know everything is either growing or dying...there is no in between! Today we know tomorrow isn't promised to anyone and today is all that we have. Today we know what we want, why we want it and when we want it by. Today we have purpose, motivation and drive. Today we have a plan. Today we live with passion!

*Principle- Everything is either growing or dying...there is no in between!

Today is the first day of the rest of our lives!

Pure Privilege

YESTERDAY

Yesterday food, fresh water, fresh air, housing, healthy bodies, abundance...these were our God given birthrights! After all, we always had them and, we deserved them! We lived in entitlement and expectation. When we didn't get what we wanted, when we wanted, how we wanted, we became angry, resentful and often hateful. More, more, more was our motto. It was never enough.

We let go, focused on things we could change and served others

TODAY

Today we've reopened our hearts, our minds and our eyes. Today we see people suffering worldwide without food, water, homes, health care, etc. Today we live in gratitude, humility, compassion and service; knowing everything we possess from our bodies to the air we breathe is a privilege... not a right! Today we know everything we have, right down to the socks on our feet, is pure privilege. Today we live in gratitude. Today we know when we're grateful we're rich. Today we give thanks for everything we've been so graciously given.

*Principle- Everything we've been so graciously given is pure privilege...not a right!

Today is the first day of the rest of our lives!

<u>Purpose</u>

YESTERDAY

Yesterday we lost our way. We had no purpose. We had no goals. We lived in distraction. We focused up to 90% of our thoughts on things we couldn't change. We became mice on a wheel trying to spin as fast as our friends and neighbours. Eventually we stopped asking why and just kept spinning. We swam into the nets by simply following the masses. We were stuck and didn't know how to get out.

We let go, focused on things we could change and served others

TODAY

Today our purpose is to live and serve by way of our gifts. Today our purpose is to keep an open heart and mind in order to best serve others. Today our purpose is to love and encourage others. Today our purpose is to treat others the way we want to be treated. Today our purpose is to lead by way of attraction...not promotion. Today our purpose is knowing what we want, why we want it and when we hope to achieve it by...without getting attached to the outcome! Today we know life is short, life is difficult and we can't take anything with us when we go. Today we know we roll the dice but someone or something else determines how they land. Today we believe in a power greater than ourselves. Today we know it's in giving that we receive.

*Principle- Live and serve by way of our proprietary gifts.

Today is the first day of the rest of our lives!

Rational/Irrational Thought

YESTERDAY

Yesterday we tried solving rational problems with irrational thought or irrational problems with rational thought...neither worked! Regardless of our intelligence, we couldn't find a corner in a round room!

We let go, focused on things we could change and served others

TODAY

Today we know we can't solve a rational problem with irrational thought nor can we solve an irrational problem with rational thought. Today we know we can't change the past, we can't change other people nor will we **ever** find a corner in a round room...no matter how hard we look! Today we know rational thought is coming to know life is short, life is difficult and we can't take anything with us when we go. Today we know rational thought is coming to understand we can't change the past, we can't guarantee the future and this moment is all that we have. Today we know rational thought is coming to understand the past does not equal the future unless we let it. Today we know the only people we can change is ourselves.

*Principle- Can't solve a rational problem with irrational thought; nor can we solve an irrational problem with rational thought.

Today is the first day of the rest of our lives!

Regrets

YESTERDAY

Yesterday we had regrets. Regrets kept us in guilt, shame & remorse. Regrets were the risks we never took or the risks we took that we never should have. Regrets were a gateway to suffering, mental illness and often premature death. Regrets were one of the many dangers that came from living in the past and focusing on things we couldn't change.

We let go, focused on things we could change and served others

TODAY

Today we've let go, cleared away the wreckage of our past and started today as the first day of the rest of our lives. Today we know we've all made mistakes. Today we know we've all rolled the dice but someone or something else determined how they landed. Today we've learned to accept life on life's terms. Today we've learned to accept people, places and things as they are. Today we know every adversity carries with it the seed to a greater benefit. Today we ask ourselves two key questions; can I we change it and what can I we learn from this? Today we've learned from our mistakes and focus on moving forward...not backwards. Today we know letting go, focusing on things we can change and serving others are keys to overcoming regret.

*Principle-Regrets were risks we never took or risks we took that we never should have.

Today is the first day of the rest of our lives!

Rejection

YESTERDAY

Yesterday we were deeply scarred from past rejections and failures. Fear of rejection kept us from taking risks. Sadly fear of rejection became our greatest motivator. We lived in fear. Fear drove us, directed us and controlled us. Never try never fail became our motto. We were damaged and ready to attack the first person who tried to hurt us. Our trust had been breached one too many times!

We let go, focused on things we could change and served others

TODAY

Today we know rejections are nothing more than third party actions we can't legislate or control. Today we've learned to accept people, places and things as they are. Today we focus on things we can change without getting attached to the outcome. Today we've let go of our expectations. Today we keep an open heart and mind. Today we know the only people we can change is ourselves. Today we work on smashing and deflating our ego. Today we know life is short...we're not here long! Today we know the greatest risk in life is to risk nothing!

Principle- We can't legislate 3rd party behaviour.

Today is the first day of the rest of our lives!

<u>Relationships</u>

YESTERDAY

Yesterday we were selfish, self-centred takers. It was all about us. We were incapable of taking our focus off self! We entered relationships to get...not give! When we gave, we gave to get! Giving with the intention of getting wasn't giving at all! We were sick.

We let go, focused on things we could change and served others

TODAY

Today we fellowship with likeminded givers or we walk our journey alone. Today we are very selective who we let in as it only takes one taker to destroy our lives. Today we know we must learn to love and forgive ourselves before we can love and forgive others. Today we know relationships are a place to go and give...not get! Today we treat others the way we want to be treated. Today we live by a simple motto; help each other, don't hurt each other. Today we lead with love and encouragement. Today we know trust and respect are the two essential ingredients in any relationship. Without trust and respect...there is nothing!

*Principle- Relationships are places to go to give...not to get!

Today is the first day of the rest of our lives!

Resentment

YESTERDAY

Yesterday we resented anyone we didn't agree with. If they didn't meet our expectations we resented them. If they threatened us in any way, we resented them. If they didn't say or do exactly as we wanted, when we wanted, how we wanted, we resented them. Over time we built walls of resentment around us to keep us safe. Rather than keep people out, we locked ourselves in and had no idea how to get out. Resentments often led to mental illness and premature death.

We let go, focused on things we could change and served others

TODAY

Today we know resentments are nothing more than unrealistic expectations. Today we know the moment we let go of our expectations, our resentments disappeared. Today we know resentments are like drinking poison and expecting the other person to die...it doesn't work! Today we know resentments are the #1 killer of alcoholics and addicts. Today we live and serve by way of our gifts. Today we've learned to let go and accept life on life's terms. Today we know the only people we can change is ourselves.

*Principle- Resentments are like drinking poison and expecting the other person to die...it doesn't work!

Today is the first day of the rest of our lives!

<u>Resetting Our Expectations</u>

YESTERDAY

Yesterday, money, power, greed, ego, will, pride, and self...these were the management gauges on our dashboard! As the middle class dissolved, these gauges dropped fast, leaving us in a place of fear, loss and uncertainty.

We let go, focused on things we could change and served others

TODAY

Today we've reset our expectations. Our new gauges are acceptance, gratitude, honesty, humility, compassion, mercy, kindness, love, etc. Today we know resentments are nothing more than unrealistic expectations. Today we live our lives in gratitude not entitlement. Today we live in acceptance not expectation. Today we know everything we have is a privilege not a right! Today we know those not willing to reset their expectations are sitting ducks. Today we come from a place of love and encouragement and have learned to accept life on life's terms.

*Principle- Resentments are nothing more than unrealistic expectations.

Today is the first day of the rest of our lives!

Respecting Others

YESTERDAY

Yesterday it was all about us. We had little to no respect for others if it didn't benefit us. Respect and fear were often one in the same...it was easy to respect those we feared. If they had something we wanted it was a different story!

We let go, focused on things we could change and served others

TODAY

Today we treat others the way we want to be treated. Today we live by a motto; help each other don't hurt each other. Today we keep an open heart and open mind on all subjects with all people. Today we live and serve by way of our gifts. Today we show others how to live and serve by way of their gifts. Today we lead with love and encouragement. Today we've reached out to those we had harmed and made amends to them all. Today we know it's in giving that we receive. Today we've learned to love our enemies from afar!

*Principle- Treat others the way you want to be treated.

Today is the first day of the rest of our lives!

<u>Revenge</u>

YESTERDAY

Yesterday we played God. It was our way or no way. We forced our will on others at any cost. We were completely selfish and self-centred. We were locked in entitlement and expectation. We were both the judge and jury. If those around us needed to be punished, we took it upon ourselves to do the judging, resenting and often much worse!

We let go, focused on things we could change and served others

TODAY

Today we live by a few simple principles. Today we no longer force our will on others. Today our hearts and minds are open. Today we come from a place of love and encouragement. Today we know the only people we can change is ourselves. Today we know we roll the dice but don't determine how they land. Today we've learned to accept life on life's terms. Today we no longer get attached to the outcome. Today we focus on living and serving by way of our gifts. Today we help each other not hurt each other. Today we treat others the way we want to be treated. Today we know it's in giving we receive. Today we're told even God doesn't judge people until their final day on earth...what gives us the right! Revenge...never!

*Principle- What comes around goes around.

Today is the first day of the rest of our lives!

Risks

YESTERDAY

Yesterday we took risks at others people expense or never risked anything at all. "Never try, never fail" was the motto of many as life passed them by. Many of us never understood that the real risk was risking nothing at all until we read the poem "Risks".

We let go, focused on things we could change and served others

TODAY

To laugh is to risk appearing the fool.
To weep is to risk appearing sentimental.
To reach out to another is to risk involvement.
To expose feelings is to risk exposing your true self.
To place your dreams, ideas before a crowd is to risk their loss.
To love is risk not being loved in return.
To live is to risk dying.
To hope is to risk despair.
To try is to risk failure.
But risks must be taken because the greatest hazard in life is to risk nothing.
The person who risks nothing, does nothing, has nothing, and is nothing.
They may avoid suffering and sorrow, but they cannot learn, feel,
change, grow, love, and live.
Chained by their certitudes, they are a slave; they have forfeited their
freedom. Only a person who risks is truly free.

*Principle- Only a person who risks is truly free.

Today is the first day of the rest of our lives!

S.L.I.P.

YESTERDAY

Yesterday we made poor choices. When they didn't turn out, we blamed others or had excuses. For many we ran to drugs and alcohol. Every time we used substances to escape from our problems, we called it a slip from our sobriety. We reasoned and justified our slips. Others told us slips were a part of recovery so we continued slipping. After all, it was accepted as a part of the process...why not slip?

We let go, focused on things we could change and served others

TODAY

Today we know slip stands for "something lousy I planned". Today we know we are responsible. Today we know we have a choice. Today we know we can change it. Today we know our old ways didn't work. Today we're sick and tired of being sick and tired. Today we'll do whatever it takes to stay sober. Today we fellowship with positive, likeminded givers. Today we know it only takes one taker to destroy our lives. Today we've let go. Today we focus on things we can change. Today we know taking focus off self and serving others are key to long term sobriety.

*Principle- S.L.I.P="Something lousy I planned"...we are responsible!

Today is the first day of the rest of our lives!

<u>Smashing Ego</u>

YESTERDAY

Yesterday self-will ran riot. It was all about us. Over time we became selfish, self-centred takers. Those who couldn't serve us had little to no value. One day life turned on us. Ego and self-will drove us to the floor. Peace and joy had left us. Focus on self had become the root cause of all our problems. We had no idea what happened or how to disengage. We became our own worst enemy.

We let go, focused on things we could change and served others

TODAY

Today we know our old ways didn't work! Today we are willing to let go...absolutely. Today we know ego, will, pride and greed were the root causes of our problems. Today we work on smashing our ego and deflation through an ongoing process of rigorous self-honesty & humility. Today we live and serve by way of our gifts. Today we focus on serving others...not self-service! Today we believe there is a power greater than ourselves at work...it's not all about us! Today we've learned to disengage. Today we feel a level of peace and serenity like never before. Today we know the only people we can change is ourselves.

*Principle- Religious doctrines worldwide share the same root message... "surrender your will or perish".

Today is the first day of the rest of our lives!

<u>Spirit</u>

YESTERDAY

Yesterday we knew Spirit was a man-made religious word. It had no value. It couldn't be seen. It couldn't be proven. Anyone who believed in spirituality was a weak minded religious fanatic we had to avoid at all costs.

We let go, focused on things we could change and served others

TODAY

Today we know wind, vibration & frequencies exist yet can't be seen. Today we know electrons, protons and DNA exist within the body yet can't be seen. Today we know universal laws and principles exist that keep the earth spinning around the sun and the earth from spinning off its axis yet they can't be seen. Today we know invisible forces are at work everywhere yet can't be seen. Today we've reopened our hearts and minds, like little children, to the ides of spirit, energy and intelligent design.

*Principle- Invisible forces are at work everywhere.

Today is the first day of the rest of our lives!

STEP 1
"LETTING GO OF THE THINGS WE CAN'T CHANGE"

PAST- BELIEFS, BEHAVIOURS, HABITS & ACTIONS WE MUST LET GO OF:

1)_____ 2)_____ 3)_____
4)_____ 5)_____ 6)_____
7)_____ 8)_____ 9)_____
10)_____ 11)_____ 12)_____
13)_____ 14)_____ 15)_____

PAST - RELATIONSHIPS, RESENTMENTS, EXPECTATIONS & ENTITLEMENTS WE MUST LET GO OF:

1)_____ 2)_____ 3)_____
4)_____ 5)_____ 6)_____
7)_____ 8)_____ 9)_____
10)_____ 11)_____ 12)_____
13)_____ 14)_____ 15)_____

PAST- UNHEALTHY PEOPLE, PLACES AND THINGS WE MUST LET GO OF:

1)_____ 2)_____ 3)_____
4)_____ 5)_____ 6)_____
7)_____ 8)_____ 9)_____
10)_____ 11)_____ 12)_____
13)_____ 14)_____ 15)_____

PAST- PEOPLE WE MUST REACH OUT TO AND LET KNOW WE'RE SORRY:

1)_____ 2)_____ 3)_____
4)_____ 5)_____ 6)_____
7)_____ 8)_____ 9)_____
10)_____ 11)_____ 12)_____
13)_____ 14)_____ 15)_____

PROMISE- I promise to work on letting go of the things I can't change and focusing on the things I can change.

Name:_____

Signature:_____ Date:_____

STEP 2
"FOCUSING ON THINGS WE CAN CHANGE"

Where am I today? (MUST GET RIGOROUSLY HONEST)

1)_____ 2)_____ 3)_____
4)_____ 5)_____ 6)_____
7)_____ 8)_____ 9)_____
10)_____ 11)_____ 12)_____
13)_____ 14)_____ 15)_____

Where do I want to be and by when? (GET ABSOLUTELY CLEAR)

1)_____ 2)_____ 3)_____
4)_____ 5)_____ 6)_____
7)_____ 8)_____ 9)_____
10)_____ 11)_____ 12)_____
13)_____ 14)_____ 15)_____

What changes and new choices must I make starting today?

1)_____ 2)_____ 3)_____
4)_____ 5)_____ 6)_____
7)_____ 8)_____ 9)_____
10)_____ 11)_____ 12)_____
13)_____ 14)_____ 15)_____

What will happen if I don't start making these changes?

1)_____ 2)_____ 3)_____
4)_____ 5)_____ 6)_____
7)_____ 8)_____ 9)_____
10)_____ 11)_____ 12)_____
13)_____ 14)_____ 15)_____

PROMISE- I promise to continue to make small changes to improve the course of my life.

Name: _____ Signature:_____

Date:_____

STEP 3
"SERVING BY WAY OF OUR GIFTS"

Please Select Your Gifts

☐ <u>Administration</u>: To have a clear vision of immediate and long-range goals and the ability to devise and execute effective plans for the accomplishment of those goals.

☐ <u>Attraction</u>: To lead by way of demonstration/attraction, not promotion.

☐ <u>Director</u>: To assume long-term personal responsibility for the welfare of a group of people.

☐ <u>Discernment</u>: To distinguish truth from untruth.

☐ <u>Exhortation</u>: To communicate step by step plans encouraging others to respond to truth in their lives.

☐ <u>Faith</u>: To discern with extraordinary confidence.

☐ <u>Giving</u>: To have the gift of giving and contribution.

☐ <u>Healing</u>: To help cure illness and restore health by way of nature, energy and vibration.

☐ <u>Helper</u>: To invest personal talents for the benefit of others.

☐ <u>Hospitality</u>: To make people feel warm and welcome.

☐ <u>Knowledge</u>: To research, analyze and systemize truth for the benefit of others.

☐ <u>Leadership</u>: To motivate others to work together.

☐ <u>Mentor</u>: To share personal gifting's with others.

☐ <u>Mercy</u>: To exhibit genuine empathy, love and compassion for those in need.

☐ <u>Messenger</u>: To exercise helpful leadership over a number of groups in spiritual matters which are spontaneously recognized and appreciated by those groups.

☐ <u>Prophet</u>: To communicate an immediate message with authority and urgency.

☐ <u>Service</u>: To serve, often making use of available resources to meet the needs of others.

☐ <u>Teacher</u>: Clearly and easily communicating quantifiable principles and processes to others.

☐ <u>Voluntary Poverty</u>: To renounce material comfort and luxury and adopt a personal lifestyle equivalent to those living at the poverty level in a given society in order to serve more effectively.

☐ <u>Wisdom</u>: To apply simple spiritual truth in everyday life.

<u>Top 5 Spiritual Gifts... In Order!</u>

1._____
2._____
3._____
4._____
5._____

Stop/Think

YESTERDAY

Yesterday our minds raced. We couldn't slow them down. We couldn't focus. We were constantly distracted. Inability to focus led to diluted thoughts, diluted actions, diluted habits and diluted lives. Inability to focus led to irrational thinking. Irrational thinking often led to addiction, depression and premature death.

We let go, focused on things we could change and served others

TODAY

Today we've let go and started today as the first day of the rest of our lives. Today we've set new goals and benchmarks. Today we no longer carry the heavy burden of yesterday. Today we understand habits are nothing more than actions without thought. Today we know changing our thoughts changes our actions which changes our lives. Today we understand the importance of stopping and thinking before we act. Today we take the time to slow down and get still often, by way of meditation and prayer. Today we understand the importance of daily fellowship with healthy, likeminded individuals. Today we know obstacles are what we see when we take our eyes off our goals. Today we stop and think!

*Principle- Stop & Think!

Today is the first day of the rest of our lives!

Success

YESTERDAY

Yesterday we measured success in money, power, and materialism. What did we have? How much did we have? How many new material possessions could we acquire? More, more, more...it was never enough! It was every man for himself!

We let go, focused on things we could change and served others

TODAY

Today success is measured by giving...not getting! Today we know self-serving only led to misery and self-destruction. Today we measure success in many different ways starting with contribution, peace, joy, happiness, good health & deep connections and relationships. Today we know it's in giving that we receive. Today we know the only things we get to keep are the things we give away. Today we know when our hearts and minds connect we experience peace like never before. Today we've come to learn our gifts and live and serve by way of our gifts. Today we know when we're grateful we're rich!

*Principle- It's in giving that we receive!

Today is the first day of the rest of our lives!

Surrender Your Will or Perish!

YESTERDAY

Yesterday "surrender" wasn't in our vocabulary. We refused to disengage or let go. We had to be right. Being right was more important than being happy. We forced our will on everyone. We did what we wanted, when we wanted how we wanted. It was all about us. Anyone in the way was the enemy. Our behaviours left us empty, angry, resentful and often destructive. We tried letting go but half measures availed us nothing.

We let go, focused on things we could change and served others

TODAY

Today we know most major religions worldwide carry one simple message...surrender your will or perish! Today we know many of the world's largest self-help groups, including Alcoholics Anonymous, carry one simple message...surrender your will or perish! Today we know forcing our will on others didn't work. Today we've surrendered our will knowing we may throw the dice but certainly don't determine how they land. Today we've come to believe in a power greater than ourselves. Today evidence of an intelligent designer is overwhelming. Today we experience levels of peace and joy we never thought possible. Today we focus on serving others...not just self! Today it's about being happy...not being right!

*Principle- We must let go... absolutely!

Today is the first day of the rest of our lives!

<u>The Right Path</u>

YESTERDAY

Yesterday we fed our bad dog a steady diet of negativity. Toxic foods, toxic people, toxic substances, violent programming, violent games, pornography...we couldn't understand why our lives were toxic!

We let go, focused on things we could change and served others

TODAY

Today we know healthy thoughts lead to healthy actions and habits which lead to healthy lives. Today we feed the good dog a steady diet of alkaline foods, loving relationships, healthy programming, etc. Today we know the dog we feed is the dog that grows. Today we know it all starts with healthy thoughts. Today we know whatever we focus on we move towards. Today we know thoughts become things. Today we know what we want, why we want them and when we want them by. Today we live and serve by way of our gifts. Today we know obstacles are what we see when we take our eyes off our goals. Today we know it only takes one bad influence to destroy our entire lives.

*Principle- The dog we feed is the dog that grows.

Today is the first day of the rest of our lives!

<u>Thoughts</u>

YESTERDAY

Yesterday many of us focused up to 90% of our thoughts on things we couldn't change. Our thinking became the root cause of our problems. Our inability or unwillingness to let go of our old ways kept us drowning at the bottom. We refused to let go. We could no longer hold on...we were stuck!

We let go, focused on things we could change and served others

TODAY

Today we know thoughts become things. Today we know whatever we focus on we move towards. Today we know our thoughts direct our actions which direct our lives. Today we know our thoughts are the rudders that guide us through life. Today we are very careful what we focus on. Today we choose to focus on the top 10% in every situation...not the bottom 10%. Today we focus on things we can change vs. things we can't. Today we know a healthy mind starts with a healthy body. Today we've simply let go of our old thinking, cleared away the wreckage of our past and started today as the first day of the rest of our lives.

*Principle- Whatever we focus on we move towards.

Today is the first day of the rest of our lives!

<u>Throwing Dice</u>

YESTERDAY

Yesterday we rolled the dice of life expecting them to land favourably. When they didn't, we grew angry, resentful, depressed...we felt a sense of entitlement! After all, we always got what we wanted...why should it stop now? The illusion of control is just that...an illusion!

We let go, focused on things we could change and served others

TODAY

Today we know we're powerless over our births, our deaths and most things in between. Today we know we throw the dice but someone or something else determines how they land. Today we know life is short, life is difficult and we can't take anything with us when we go. Today we know we can't change the past, we can't guarantee the future and this moment is all that we have. Today we focus on things we can change WITHOUT GETTING ATTACHED TO THE OUTCOME. Today we've learned to accept life on life's terms...not our terms! Today we've let go and come to believe in a power greater than ourselves. Today we share this simple dice metaphor with everyone we know.

*Principle- We roll the dice but don't determine how they land.

Today is the first day of the rest of our lives!

Thy Will Not Mine

YESTERDAY

Yesterday it was our way or no way. It was all about us. We forced our will on everyone. We rationalized, justified and reasoned if it meant getting what we wanted. We kept our hearts and minds closed unless there was something in it for us. We were sick! Self-will had run riot.

We let go, focused on things we could change and served others

TODAY

Today scientific evidence of intelligent design is overwhelming. Today we've come to believe in a power greater than ourselves. Today we've learned to accept life on life's terms. Today we've come to realize we roll the dice but someone or something else determines how they land. Today we know our birth, our death and most circumstances in between are beyond our control. Today we experience peace and joy like never before. Today we know we can't live in fear and faith at the same time. Today we live and serve by way of our gifts. Today we've let of our old ways absolutely; knowing they didn't work!

*Principle- Can't be in fear and faith at the same time.

Today is the first day of the rest of our lives!

Time with Self

YESTERDAY

Yesterday life got busy. We were distracted. Family, work, television, internet...we were in constant overwhelm. Overwhelm often led to irrational thought. Irrational thought often led to irrational actions. We made poor choices. Before long life was on top of us. We had no idea how we got here or how to crawl out. We were stuck.

We let go, focused on things we could change and served others

TODAY

Today we start each morning reviewing our steps and giving thanks for all the wonderful gifts we've been given; from the water we drink, to the air we breathe, to the beautiful people we have in our lives. Today we start each morning focusing on where we're going and how we're getting there, knowing obstacles are what we see when we take our eyes off our goals. Today we know starting each day in gratitude and visualization is the secret to a happy, healthy life. Today we take the time each morning to get quiet and give thanks for all that we have.

Principle- Starting each day in gratitude and visualization is the secret to a happy, healthy life.

Today is the first day of the rest of our lives!

Tomorrow Never Comes

YESTERDAY

Yesterday we procrastinated. We put things off until tomorrow. Soon "tomorrow" became a code word for never. New problems continued to arise daily making it impossible to deal with the problems of yesterday. Soon we had a mountain of things to do and no time to do them. We trained ourselves to procrastinate and couldn't understand why we were buried. Our lives seemed hopeless. We were stuck!

We let go, focused on things we could change and served others

TODAY

Today we've cleared away the wreckage of our past, let go and started today as the first day of the rest of our lives. Today we're no longer distracted by the things we can't change. Today we have time to deal with things we can change. Today we know what we want, why we want it and when we want it by. Today we live in the moment knowing the future isn't promised to anyone. Today we live life to the fullest. Today we know it's not just the length of our life that counts...it's the width!

*Principle- Tomorrow isn't promised to anyone.

Today is the first day of the rest of our lives!

<u>Torment</u>

YESTERDAY

Yesterday we focused on things we couldn't change over long periods of time. This led to torment, feelings of insanity and often premature death. Our hearts and minds became disconnected. Our behaviours and beliefs ran counter to one another. Our selfish, self-centered ways drove us away from love and connection. We focused on things we couldn't change so long, rational and irrational thought became one in the same. We lived in confusion and torment!

We let go, focused on things we could change and served others

TODAY

Today we know when we let go of things we can't change we experience peace. Today we know when we detach from an outcome we experience peace. Today we know when we live and serve by way of our gifts we experience peace. Today we know when we accept life on life's terms we find peace. Today we know when our hearts and minds align we experience peace. Today we know when our behaviours and beliefs are one in the same we experience peace. Today we know when we get still we experience peace. Today we know we roll the dice but don't determine how they land. Today we experience peace like never before. Today we know life is short, life is difficult and we can't take anything with us when we go.

*Principle- Today we accept life on life's terms.

Today is the first day of the rest of our lives!

Trust & Respect

YESTERDAY

Yesterday our trust and respect had been breached by friends, family, partners, co-workers, institutions, corporations...the list went on. We were deeply scarred. Our trust was at an all-time low. It seemed as though trust and respect took a back seat to pride, ego, will and greed if we wanted to get ahead. If we couldn't beat them, we had to join them...we were miserable.

We let go, focused on things we could change and served others

TODAY

Today we've cleared away the wreckage of our past and started today as the first day of the rest of our lives. Today we live and serve by way of our gifts. Today we treat others the way we want to be treated. Today we live by a simple motto; help each other don't hurt each other. Today we know trust and respect are the two most important components in any healthy relationship. Today we chose to be givers...not takers! Today we know it's in giving that we receive.

*Principle- Trust and respect are the two most important principles in any healthy relationship.

Today is the first day of the rest of our lives!

Value of Adversity

YESTERDAY

Yesterday we took the wrong path. We made the wrong choices. We let the wrong people in. We crossed lines we never thought we would cross. Premature death was inevitable.

We let go, focused on things we could change and served others

TODAY

Today we can relate to those who have fallen when others can't. Today we can share our experience, strength and hope where others can't. Today we know yesterday's worst offenders are often today's most influential leaders when serving. Today we know there are few lessons in success. Today we've found the right path by exhausting the wrong ones. Today we know every adversity carries with it the seed to a greater benefit. Today we know success comes from making the right decisions, making the right decisions comes from experience and experience comes from making the wrong decisions. Yesterday's liabilities are our largest assets when serving others...who ever would of thought!

*Principle- Every adversity carries with it the seed to a greater benefit.

Today is the first day of the rest of our lives!

Visualization

YESTERDAY

Yesterday life came at us fast and furious and we were in constant reaction. Jobs, bills, responsibilities, and pressures...it just kept coming. Eventually we were in over our heads trying to catch our tail. Staying on top became a futile exercise. Hopelessness and depression set in for some. Anger, frustration and aggression set in for others. We were no longer controlling our destiny... someone else was doing it for us! We were stuck on the carousel and had no idea how to get off. We were no longer on top of things... they were on top of us.

We let go, focused on things we could change and served others

TODAY

Today we've found the courage to let go and start over. Today we've learned our gifts and how to best serve others by way of these gifts. Today we know exactly what we want, how we plan to get it and when we're going to achieve it by. Today we know thoughts become things. Today we know whatever we focus on we move towards. Today we know what the mind can believe, the mind can achieve! Today we know obstacles are what we see when we take our eyes off our goals. Today we focus on and attract the things we want...not more of the things we don't want!

*Principle- We'll see it when we believe it!

Today is the first day of the rest of our lives!

<u>We Don't Know It!</u>

YESTERDAY

Yesterday we had all the answers. We read all the books. We had acquired all the knowledge. No one knew what we had been through. We had enough experience to mentor everyone. Unfortunately we preached one message and demonstrated another.

We let go, focused on things we could change and served others

TODAY

Today we know if we're not doing it, we don't know it! Today we lead by example. Today we practice what we preach. Today we lead by way of attraction...not promotion. Today we show others...not tell others! Today we know preaching one message and demonstrating another is called lying. Today we know what we want. Today we know what new choices we need to make to get there. Today we know our gifts and how to apply them.

*Principle- Actions speak louder than words...just do it!

Today is the first day of the rest of our lives!

We're All Sick

YESTERDAY

Yesterday we were selfish, self-centered takers. Our hearts and minds were closed. We focused on things we couldn't change. We preached one message and demonstrated another. We entered relationships to get...not give! If we gave, we gave to get. We lived in expectation and entitlement...we had rights! We focused on the bottom 10%...not the top 10%. We took everyone else's inventory...never our own! We were toxic. We were very sick.

We let go, focused on things we could change and served others

TODAY

Today we let go absolutely, completed our 3 steps and started today as the first day of the rest of our lives. Today we keep it simple. Today we live with an open heart and mind. Today we live one day at a time. Today we start each day in gratitude for what we have. Today we accept life on life's terms knowing although we roll the dice we certainly don't determine how they land. Today we've learned to live and serve by way of our gifts. Today we know the only people we can change is ourselves. Today we've forgiven ourselves and others. Today we know we're all sick...some sicker than others. Today we work towards progress...not perfection!

*Principle- We're all sick...some sicker than others!

Today is the first day of the rest of our lives!

What Can We Learn From This?

YESTERDAY

Yesterday we all made mistakes...some more than others. We were all sick....some sicker than others. Life was often unkind. We lived through more trauma than most. For many, bad luck surrounded us. Why did all this misfortune have to happen to us?

We let go, focused on things we could change and served others

TODAY

Today we ask ourselves the two most important questions several times each day. Question #1 is; can I change it? Question #2 is; what can I learn from this? These two questions have changed our lives. Today we know there are few lessons in success. Today we know few things ever happen so bad we can't either laugh at it or learn something from it. Today we know we often find the right path by exhausting the wrong ones. Today we know every adversity carries with it the seed to a greater benefit. Today, no matter how bad the situation, we can ask ourselves, what can we learn from this? Today we know success comes from making the right decision, the right decision comes from experience, and experience comes from making the wrong decision. Today we know asking these two questions again and again can only lead to wisdom.

Principle- The two most important questions we must ask ourselves daily- Question #1 is; Can I Change It? Question #2 is; What can I learn from this?

Today is the first day of the rest of our lives!

When We Mess Up

YESTERDAY

Yesterday we hid our mistakes. We refused to admit we were wrong. We became experts at lying to others but couldn't lie to ourselves. How could we trust anybody else if we didn't trust ourselves? Guilt, shame and remorse soon followed. To redirect blame, we took everyone else's inventory...never our own!

We let go, focused on things we could change and served others

TODAY

Today we know rigorous self-honesty saved us from our past. Today when we mess up we're the first to admit it. Today we know we can find the right paths by exhausting the wrong ones. Today our biggest assets were yesterday's biggest liabilities when serving others. Today experience and wisdom are our greatest gifts. Today we know there are few lessons in success. Today we focus on taking our own inventory. Today we know the only people we can change is ourselves.

*Principle- Experience and wisdom are our greatest gifts.

Today is the first day of the rest of our lives!

Who Can We Change?

YESTERDAY

Yesterday we spent as much as 90% of our time focusing on things we couldn't change. Past events, television, internet, fiction, sporting events, other people...we were distracted. We were busy taking everyone else's inventory while our own lives were in turmoil. We were stuck and didn't even know it.

We let go, focused on things we could change and served others

TODAY

Today we focus on things we can change. Today we know the only people we can change is ourselves. Today we know exactly what we want, why we want it and when we hope to achieve it by. Today we make small changes each day that impact our lives significantly. Today we've simply changed our core thoughts and beliefs which have changed our actions, habits and the course of our lives.

*Principle- Who can we change...just ourselves!

Today is the first day of the rest of our lives!

<u>Willingness</u>

YESTERDAY

Yesterday our hearts and minds were closed. We listened if it benefitted us. Not only were we not willing to listen to others...we forced our will on them! It was simply our way or no way. Our walls were up and no one was getting through.

We let go, focused on things we could change and served others

TODAY

Today we are willing to let go absolutely. Today we are willing to focus on things we can change without getting attached to the outcome. Today we are willing to serve others by way of our gifts. Today we are willing to get rigorously self-honest with ourselves. Today we are willing to open our hearts and minds to infinite possibilities. Today we are willing to get still and listen. Today we are willing to help each other...not hurt each other. Today we are willing to treat others the way we want to be treated. Today we are willing to love our enemies from afar.

Principle- A willing heart and mind is an open heart and mind.

Today is the first day of the rest of our lives!

<u>Worry</u>

YESTERDAY

Yesterday we lived in fear, worry, guilt and shame. We worried about things we had done. We worried about things we hadn't done. We were scared to live and scared to die. We continually focused on things we couldn't change. We were sick. We were stuck.

We let go, focused on things we could change and served others

TODAY

Today we've let go absolutely, knowing life is short, life is difficult and we can't take anything with us when we go. Today we know we can't change the past nor guarantee the future...today is all that we have! Today we've let go of our expectations. Today we've learned to accept life on life's terms. Today we accept people, places and things as they are knowing the only people we can change is ourselves. Today we live and serve by way of our gifts. Today we know we roll the dice but someone or something else determines how they land. Today we know we can't live in fear and faith at the same time. Today we know we can't be grateful and depressed at the same time. Today we know the only thing to fear is fear itself! Today we know when we're grateful we're rich!

*Principle- The only thing to fear is fear itself!

Today is the first day of the rest of our lives!

What Did We Learn From This Book?

- Life is short (we're not here long)
- Life is difficult (every moment is a privilege...not a right!)
- We can't take anything with us when we go (everything decays)
- We can't change the past (it's gone forever)
- We can't guarantee the future (tomorrow isn't promised to anyone)
- Today is all that we have (live in the now)
- Only people we can change is ourselves (we can't force lasting change on others)
- The past doesn't equal the future unless we let it (today is first day of the rest...)
- Today is the first day of the rest of our lives (resetting our lives is paramount)
- We roll the dice, but don't determine how they land (power greater than ourselves)
- We're powerless over most things in our lives (forces beyond our control exist)
- Let go of the things we can't change (can I change it?)
- Focus on things we can change (can I change it?)
- We possess proprietary gifts (why weren't we taught these?)
- We must live and serve by way of these gifts (purpose, fulfillment and destiny)
- Acceptance and serving others is the secret to a happy life (in giving we receive)
- Honesty leads to humility...humility leads to freedom (rigorous honesty is key)
- Smashing ego and deflation is critical (surrendering your will is mandatory)
- When we're grateful, we're rich (focus on the top 10%...not the bottom 10%)
- Must reopen our eyes, hearts and minds (knowing our old ways didn't work)
- Must never get attached to the outcome (don't force our will on others)
- When it comes to God...further diligence is necessary (DNA is a blueprint)
- Evidence of an intelligent designer is overwhelming (blueprint requires a designer)
- Everything we've been given is a privilege, not a right (every moment is s gift)
- Good and bad dog exist in us all. (dog we feed is the one that grows)
- Love with conditions is control (must learn to love unconditionally)
- Depression is a luxury (have to have it real good to know how bad we have it)
- Ego is pride in forward...depression is pride in reverse (must take focus off self)
- Serving others is the cure all (addiction, entitlement, depression, anxiety, etc.)
- Can't be half pregnant (we must commit)
- What can I learn from this? (#2 question we must ask on a regular basis)
- No one cares how much we know until they know how much we care (must care)
- Progress is the key...not perfection (slow and steady)
- Principles before personalities (must put principles before personalities)
- Routine is a key to a happy life (balance and harmony require moderation)
- Getting still leads to inspiration (must empty our glass before refilling)
- Giving to get isn't giving (must give unconditionally)
- Our enemies are often our greatest teachers (learn to love our enemies from afar)

Feel free to contact us at: www.canichangeit.com

Today is the first day of the rest of our lives!

*** *The 12 Promises of Alcoholics Anonymous*

If we are painstaking about this phase of our development we will be amazed before we are half way through.

(1) We are going to know a new freedom and a new happiness.

(2) We will not regret the past nor wish to shut the door on it.

(3) We will comprehend the word serenity and we will know peace.

(4) No matter how far down the scale we have gone, we will see how our experience can benefit others.

(5) That feeling of uselessness and self-pity will disappear.

(6) We will lose interest in selfish things and gain interest in our fellows.

(7) Self-seeking will slip away.

(8) Our whole attitude and outlook upon life will change.

(9) Fear of people and of economic insecurity will leave us.

(10) We will intuitively know how to handle situations which used to baffle us.

(11) We will suddenly realize that God is doing for us what we could not do for ourselves.

(12) Are these extravagant promises? We think not. They are being fulfilled among us sometimes quickly, sometimes slowly. They will always materialize if we work for them.